Manchester Memories

The publishers would like to thank the following companies for their

support in the production of this book

Main Sponsor
G H Sheldon Wholesale Bakers Limited

A & S Domestic

Austin Trumanns Steel

Roland Bardsley Construction

Donald Brown

Donns Solicitors

Colgate Palmolive

G-MEX Centre

James Halstead

Harvitool

KB Group of Companies

Independent Order of Oddfellows

Manchester Grammar School

JH Miller & Sons

R Noone & Son Limited

Packaging Products Limited

Procter & Gamble Product Supply (UK) Limited

Poppleton & Appleby

Regatta Limited

Rolls-Royce

GE Sparkes

Stax Trade Centre

Sub Soil Surveys Limited

Temperature Controls

UMIST

Unilever Bestfoods

Withington Girls' School

White Reclamations

First published in Great Britain by True North Books Limited

England HX3 6AE

01422 344344

ISBN 1 903204 54 2

Text, design and origination by True North Books Limited

Printed and bound by The Amadeus Press Limited

Manchester Memories

Contents

Introduction

'Manchester Memories' is a wonderful opportunity to dip into the past and indulge in nostalgia. Within these pages are glorious photographs of the city as we remember it from our childhood or as our parents and grandparents described. Each image is accompanied by a caption that helps further to bring those memories to life. Every one adds something to the photograph that will inform, entertain or provoke a reaction. We all have our own opinions of life as it was in the last century and this book can help firm up our prejudices or, just perhaps, make us rethink those views. But this collection is not intended to be dry and dusty, more a cheery dip into the days that made us what we are and a reminder of buildings, streets and activities that have passed into the data bank of history. Yet, for those of us who lived though that period there is so much that we would like to recall. We cannot bring back the past, but this is an opportunity to revisit the face of the city that has

had its plastic surgery in modern times. Perhaps we have forgotten how it once looked, so this is a guaranteed opportunity to peel back the layers and roll back the years. Not everything on our nostalgic journey through the middle years of the 20th century is covered with joy and happiness. There is war, grime, poverty and heartache along the way and these must be encountered so that we can better appreciate the happier times that have come our way. Thankfully, they outweigh the bad times and 'Manchester Memories' makes no excuse for reminding us of them over and over again. Ours is a fine city with an impressive past that is to be celebrated. As the reader moves through the pages personal memories will come flooding back. Some will be mundane but others will have a personal significance. Each of us will find something different to recall from each delightful image or wry and poignant caption. It is also an excellent chance to involve younger readers by including them in this amble along memory lane for it is important that they appreciate what

Families eagerly await the arrival of HRH Princess Margaret in 1950.

it was that we held dear.

Manchester has not always held the place of prominence in Britain that it now holds. There was little life to be seen in AD 79 when the Romans built a fort on the Irwell, in the vicinity of the present Castlefield, that they called Mancunium or Mamuciam, meaning 'breast shaped hill'. After the Romans left the fort and town, various tribes of Angles, Saxons and Danes took turns in a mixture of raiding and settling here. By the time of the Norman conquest Mameceaster, as it had become known, had developed a second centre of population around the cathedral. In these early times Salford was much more important and the village we now know as Manchester was just a small part of that larger town. It began to grow in importance as a market town in medieval times and its increasing influence was recognised by the grant of an annual fair at Acresfield in 1222. The infant textile industry developed near Hanging Ditch and was helped to grow with the arrival of Flemish weavers fleeing religious persecution in their homeland.

The town's modest place on the country's ladder of influence helped it to avoid becoming a battle-ground during the Wars of the Roses but, because of its staunch support for Parliament in the Civil War, Royalist forces laid siege to the town in 1642. However, the defences were so strong that they gave up and later sacked Bolton instead! At this time the name of Manchester was not yet of national significance. It was still no more than a market town and by 1717 its population was a mere 10,000. But change was in the air. The second half of the 18th century would herald the rise in Manchester's glory that would bring international recognition to what had once been a tiny hamlet on the banks of a little known river. For Manchester was to become an urban prototype as, in many respects, it could claim to be the first of the new generation of huge industrial cities created in the western world during the past 250 years. The opening of the Duke of Bridgewater Canal, so that coal could be transported easily and cheaply, opened the floodgates of the industrial revolution. The invention of steam powered machines for use in the textile business led to large factories and warehouses appearing. By the turn into the 19th century Manchester was the cotton king, making huge fortunes for merchants and factory owners. The population leapt from 25,000 in 1772 to a figure nearly four times larger in less than 30 years.

The coming of the railway age added to Manchester's importance as the town was in the

The majestic Albert Memorial in Albert Square, pictured in 1950.

vanguard of modern transport development. The Duke of Wellington presided at the opening of the line to Liverpool in 1830, though the ceremony was tainted by demonstrations against the prime minister who was linked with the deaths of people killed in the Peterloo massacre 11 years before. By this time the population stood at over 250,000 and the rest of the 19th century would see a rise to the economic heights the like of which had not been seen before. It continued into the years before the Great War as the Lancashire cotton industry became responsible for producing almost two thirds of the world's output. But a lack of investment in modern equipment and cheaper labour overseas saw markets begin to shrink and cotton declined and was all but dead and buried by the 1950s. New industries in Trafford Park and a move towards distribution helped offset the loss of textile production.

We also lost many of our fine Victorian and Edwardian buildings to the ravages of war when Goering's Luftwaffe bombers flattened so much of the city centre and the planners of the 1960s finished off the architectural holocaust. Fortunately, 'Manchester Memories' can help undo some of the damage and revive those long lost edifices. At the same time we can dance again to the Hollies and Wayne Fontana and the Mindbenders at the Twisted Wheel or the Oasis. We can put our bikes into a back yard on Horton Road for just threepence and nip through the alleys to Maine Road and cheer another goal from Joe Hayes. Across the city others can give a tanner to a lad who will mind their Morris Cowley parked near Glover's as they crowd the Stretford End to watch David Pegg race down the left wing. At the weekend we can return to Belle Vue and ride an elephant or boo Jackie Pye in his wrestling leotard in the King's Hall. Perhaps the best way to read 'Manchester Memories' is to get into true nostalgic mood. Go to the wardrobe and select an A-line skirt or pair of drainpipe trousers. Put in a set of curlers or slick back your hair with a dab of Brylcreem. Tell the children to close their copies of 'School Friend' and 'Film Fun' and tidy away the Biggles and Famous Five books. Wind up the gramophone and put on an old 78. Anne Shelton can sing 'Arrivederci Darling' or Johnny Ray belt out 'Such a Night'. Fill the pot with some Horniman's tea and pop it under the little cosy that grandma knitted. Reach for a plateful of sugar butties and you are ready for the off. It is now the moment to return to shillings and pence, pounds and ounces and enjoy every single moment.

Events & occasions

Below: There is a touch of majesty about the sight of a detachment of mounted police riding imperiously along the road. The upright posture of both horse and rider indicates a touch of superiority in the constable and his steed. On the corner of Cobourg Street and Whitworth Street the 1936 law enforcement team was not just employed for show because there had been occasions when it was called into action. Oswald Mosley's British Union of Fascists were notorious trouble makers, stirring up feelings at rallies when tempers often got the better of normally placid souls who allowed themselves to be stirred by the rhetoric of the orator. Disaffected members of the ranks of the unemployed felt the weight of the force on horseback as their meetings were cleared when they became unruly. Manchester's police force came into being after the setting up of a Watch Committee in 1839 and an office was established on Cross Street. Manchester City Police did not take control at Southmill Street until 1937 when special laboratories for forensics, fingerprints and photography were opened. In the 1930s each horse cost £75 and by the mid 1950s there were only 19 such animals on police duty. Most of these were used in assisting officers on traffic duty. Stables and a training centre were opened at Hough End in 1976 and by 1980 there were 40 horses at the disposal of the mounted police, increasingly being used in crowd control, especially outside football grounds.

When VE Day announced the end of the war in Europe there were wild, unbridled displays of delight the length and breadth of Britain. After six years of suffering the hostilities had come to an end with Hitler committing suicide after cowering in his Berlin bunker and his cronies being rounded up ready to face trial for their crimes. There was dancing in the streets, services of celebration in the churches and mass scenes of joyous gatherings in town hall squares. Beacons blazed upon the hillsides and even on Rosamund Street, Chorlton on Medlock, the children lit their own VE bonfire to mark the momentous occasion. Mums in their floral frocks and pinnies joined in the festivities by using up jealously hoarded food coupons and splashing them on ingredients for buns and butties that formed part of the party spread when they all sat down at trestle tables in the middle of the road. They toasted the King with a utility form of orangeade and gave three cheers for good old Winnie, the country's saviour as prime minister, and whose portrait was hung as proudly as any union flag from the bunting flying above the cobbled streets. There were few men in sight to join in the party as most of them were still mopping up in Germany or fighting in the Far East, but our hearts were with them as we sang about bluebirds, white cliffs and Dover.

Above: The 1930s were a struggle for ordinary folk as wages were cut, living conditions failed to improve and unemployment rose to 3,000,000. There were pitched street battles between the police and disaffected workers and hunger marches on the capital included a Lancashire contingent in 1932. Aldous Huxley published 'Brave New World', but little could be seen of it at that time. The jobless were still marching in 1936 when men from Jarrow, a northeast town with 68 per cent of its workforce out of a job, hit the road on a five week journey. It came as no surprise to see the rise in popularity of such minor, but disruptive, political groups as the British Union of Fascists and the National Workers' Movement. The leaders of the day used a mixture of bully boy tactics and softly softly approaches to hold things in check. The Royal Family played its part by being seen to take an interest in the lives of its subjects, though from the look on the faces of these Mancunians this visit was hardly inspirational. The Prince of Wales toured Britain in the early 1930s, often concentrating on workingmen's clubs, and enlisted more than 200,000 men and women in occupational schemes. During these years his popularity rose to a level achieved by his grandfather when he held the same title. However, his star waned in 1936 when, as King Edward VIII, news of his desire to wed the twice divorced American socialite, Wallis Simpson, became public. He abdicated five months before his scheduled coronation.

Top right: When peace was declared in 1945 the blackout curtains could come down and there was an end to those wardens and their bellowing 'Turn that light out'. Beacons blazed on hilltops across the country and in city centres there were giant firework displays with rockets fizzing and sparking

as they rushed up into the night sky. Even public transport was used as way of expressing the nation's joy and brightly illuminated victory trams, looking like something purloined from the Blackpool illuminations, trundled along their tracks. Only those who lived through the dark and dismal wartime days can appreciate what it felt like to have lights gleaming in the evening once more. For nearly six years the only illumination had been provided by the bursting of shells, tracer bullets ripping through the air and the glow created by burning houses and factories after an air raid. Light had literally come back into the world and it was the herald of a bright future, or so the country hoped. In the general election that July the electorate turned to a new breed of politicians to take it forward into the second half of the century. Labour swept into power with a massive majority of 180 over the Tories. Prime Minister Attlee promised, 'We can deliver the goods.' In 1951 the public decided they hadn't and turned back to Churchill once more.

Life was tough in the 1930s for the working classes during the depression years when the country's economy struggled to make headway. Unemployment was high and wages were cut, leading to strikes, marches and a 'them and us' attitude existing between the haves and have nots. The cares of the world are etched in the face of the woman in the foreground. What a hard life she must have had. Born in the Victorian era she had been brought up in overcrowded housing that lacked proper sanitation, electricity or even the most basic living standards that we now take for granted. She had waved her husband off as he marched away to war in 1914, welcomed him back a disillusioned man after his experiences in the trenches and then tried to rebuild for a future 'fit for heroes' as the government had glibly promised. Despite all the knock backs she could still be proud to be British and a loyal supporter of the monarchy. On Malcolm Street, Clayton she and her neighbours had prepared the tables for a street party in honour of the silver jubilee celebrations for King George V. On 6 May 1935 the nation got together in the biggest demonstration of unity since Armistice Day in 1918, but once the parties were over and the decks cleared it was back to life on a shoestring.

Left: Best foot forward, ma'am, and what a pretty foot it was as well in 1950. Sadly, it was to be a part of Princess Margaret's anatomy that was to cause her great distress in the final years leading up to her death in February 2002. She scalded herself badly and, although not the cause of her death, added to her decline from the vibrant and radiant woman she had once been. This visit to Manchester was one of many ceremonial duties she began to take on as a major royal figure after the war. Her work was to become even more important and her official life much busier once her sister had acceded to the throne in 1952. Born on 21 August 1930 Princess Margaret Rose was but a slip of a young woman when she visited Manchester, yet it is obvious from the admiring glances of the men in the crowd that here was a beauty who would continue to turn heads. She was something of a rebellious and forthright person, as second children often are, and soon made her way into the gossip columns of national newspapers with her comments and social whirl. It was her affair

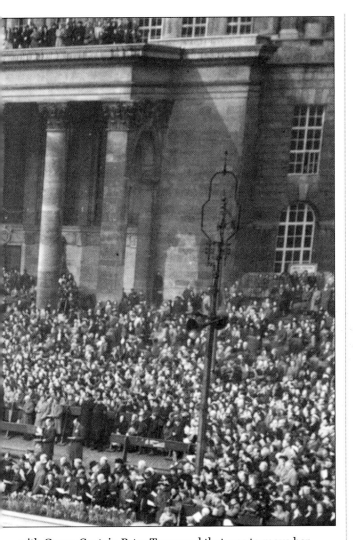

with Group Captain Peter Townsend that was to move her onto the front pages in 1955 when it seemed certain that she was going to announce marriage to her father's former equerry. He was a divorced man and the establishment feared ructions that might rival the 1936 abdication crisis. Princess Margaret eventually gave in to the pressure and severed connections with Townsend, but she never looked as happy again.

Above: After the war there was much rebuilding to be undertaken as we repaired huge tracts of land laid waste by the ravages of the bombing blitzes of the early 1940s. We also had to rebuild ourselves as a people and we took every opportunity that we could to turn out in large numbers to show solidarity. A service held at the Cenotaph was enough of a reason to come along and pay corporate respects, but this one had the added incentive of being attended by Queen Elizabeth, the mother of our present monarch. In 1949 the country was trying its best to get back to normal. Sporting venues were filled to bursting by huge crowds denied the pleasure of watching top-notch soccer, cricket and speedway for so many years. Cinemas and variety theatres were packed out once again and fairgrounds and circuses had

guaranteed support. But the war was too fresh in the memory to be ignored. Shortages of basic goods made life a struggle and our hearts still ached for those who did not make it through the dark days. Mancunians came to St Peter's Square to honour their royal guest, but mainly to remember the dead. The scene outside Central Library is a little different now since the Metrolink trams began to run past, but the Midland to the left remains. Various attempts to fiddle with this hotel's name have been made, using any permutation from Holiday Inn, Crowne Plaza and International that you can think of, but it is still the Midland Hotel to most of us.

Top: Quite what the two pianos on the stage were doing during a religious rally at Belle Vue's King's Hall in 1950 is not clear. Perhaps Rawitz and Landauer, a pair of classical musicians who were forever appearing as guests to try and add a touch of the highbrow to variety shows in the 1950s, were due to perform later the following evening. It takes all sorts and King's Hall had more than its share of mixed events and people headlining its functions. There were political rallies, festivals, conferences, variety acts, wrestling and bingo bonanzas. They all added spice to the life of the well patronised building, but the most fondly remembered occasions have to be reserved for the times when the circus performers went through their routines. Glamorous girls standing on the backs of horses galloping around the ring, lion tamers going through their death defying routines, acrobats, tightrope walkers and the trapeze artists were part of a magical show. Then there were the true speciality acts, such as Captain Harry Schmidt and Evelyn with their sealions clapping their flippers and playing tunes on horns that they honked with their snouts. How the children loved to laugh at the antics of Jacko Fossett as he clowned about for three decades until the circus closed down in 1981.

Right: Garlands, streamers and the proud flags of St George waving over King Street in 1953 heralded the coronation of 2 June 1953. Elizabeth II had come to the throne on 6 February 1952, but the country had to wait nearly 16 months for the official period of mourning to end and preparations be made for the ceremonial coronation. It was an event that had a remarkable spin off in television sales. The goggle box was still in its infancy and few households possessed one, but the BBC had overcome narrow minded resistance from the establishment and had persuaded the powers that be to allow cameras into Westminster Abbey to screen the event. From that day on the importance of radio as the main source of news and entertainment in the home was to start to decline. Neighbours who had bought a little box with its flickering black and white screen suddenly discovered that they had a host of friends on their street as people crowded into their front rooms to listen to the rich, sonorous tones of Richard Dimbleby describing the events that unfolded before him. The decorations on King Street had twice been put to good use in 1945 when we celebrated VE and VJ Day, but after Coronation Day they could be put away for another 25 years until the Silver Jubilee came along.

Below: The main shopping area on King Street is now pedestrianised with retail outlets like Monsoon, Virgin, Planet and the Body Shop attempting to attract custom. In 1953 cars could comfortably make their way along here without the restrictions that came into force in the latter decades of the 20th century. The Ford Popular and other cars were a reminder of Henry Ford's statement that customers could have any colour they wanted as long as it was black. Half a century ago we did not have the exotic shades and metallic hues available to the modern motorist. Somehow the drab colours seemed to suit the austere times, but at least there was a splash of colour in the Coronation decorations fluttering in the breeze. St George was well to the fore amongst the flowers and garlands that complemented the banners hung in celebration of that memorable day that gave the whole country a lift. Goodness how we needed it! There was a war raging in Korea, rationing for some items was still with us and the east coast had been devastated by floods. The crowning of our lovely young queen gave the whole country a lift and the celebratory mood was helped by the news that Edmund Hillary had conquered Everest. In that same year Stanley Matthews won his FA Cup medal at last, Gordon Richards at long last rode a Derby winner and our cricket team regained the Ashes.

Above: Preparations for the Queen's coronation were just about complete at the end of May 1953. Flags fluttered in the breeze in what turned out to be several days of rather unseasonable weather. When the great day dawned the rain clouds gathered but the intermittent showers did not dampen the ardour of the crowds tucked in behind the crash barriers who turned out to witness the procession through Albert Square. Down in the capital a sea of people turned out to line the route to Westminster Abbey and witness the presence of representatives from the far corners of the British Commonwealth paying homage to Her Majesty. One of the most impressive figures was that cut by Queen Salote of Tonga, a huge and beaming figure who waved vigorously to the crowds as her open carriage rapidly filled with rainwater pouring down upon her. When Dr Fisher, the Archbishop of Canterbury, placed St Edward's Crown upon our new sovereign's head he must have said his own silent prayer of good luck for the 27 year old who was setting off on a royal voyage that the nation hoped would bring Britain into a new Elizabethan age. The monarch had inherited a country still suffering the economic effects of an expensive war and her subjects dearly wished that with her accession we would all be able to move forward into the better times that lay ahead.

Centre: At Kendal's, Santa Claus had a better class of Christmas present in his grotto than most other department stores, though it cost mum and dad a bit extra for the privilege. That probably did not mean too much because you needed a few bob to your name in 1953 to be able to do much more than browse through the various floors before settling for a cup of coffee. Even that was served at greater than Kardomah prices. Kendal Milne was largely reserved for the middle classes in those days, the sort of people who cried 'mansion!' when they filled a bingo card. The average man's weekly wage was about £10 and that of his wife just half of that. The clientele became more varied as greater spending power was more widely available in later years, but the store still retained a certain status. In recent years, however, it has lost some of its independent feel as other retail outlets have taken over some of the space behind its sweeping frontage. Kendal, Milne and Faulkner were partners in the middle of the 19th century, beginning in business when they bought a shopping bazaar from S & J Watts in 1836. The partnership originally concentrated on silks, but when Faulkner died in 1862 his name was dropped and in 1870 Kendal Milne opened on Deansgate. Lewis's was to be one of its main rivals, but at this stage of its trading history Kendal Milne concentrated on drapery and furniture, leaving Lewis's to develop its clothing sales.

The Whit Walks were a tradition that brought even the greatest of cities to a standstill. Marching bands led the way and church groups unfurled their banners and the faithful proudly walked along behind. In Market Street in 1955 even office workers in the Exchange buildings put their pens to one side and looked down upon the delightful parade heading towards them. The pavement was covered by a seething mass of people who took great pleasure in the spectacle and proud mums joined in by walking with their little ones so beautifully dressed for the occasion. Garlands of flowers, little posies and pretty headdresses all added to the sense of pageantry. The girls held on to their streamers as some tried to perform a sort of maypole dance as they went along. It usually ended in confusion, but what did it matter? Everyone enjoyed the day and that was the main purpose of the walks. Traditionally, children all got new clothes and after they had finished their procession the youngsters went off to visit an old auntie or uncle they had not seen for ages, hopeful of a small addition to their piggy banks. 'Must be Whitsun, then', muttered one grumpy relative as he answered the door being pounded by an eager little tot. On returning home the new outfits were put away for use on future high days and holidays.

Below: In 1958 Jane Morgan sang about the day that the rains came down. Perhaps the composer had passed through Albert Square three years earlier and witnessed this scene. When Queen Elizabeth II made her 1955 visit to our city the greeting may have been warm but the day was decidedly horrid. But it did not dampen the spirits of the largely female crowd that turned out to welcome its royal guest. Long calf length coats, pacamacs, rainhoods and brollies were the fashion order of the day. It says much for both Mancunian loyalty to the crown and typical northern determination that so many braved the elements to cheer a young monarch, still in her 20s. There was a touch of glamour about the Queen, something we had not seen in her shy father. She was also a woman who needed our support, thrust into the forefront of public attention at such a tender age when George VI died in 1952. Queen Elizabeth attracted crowds like some modern pop star and, wherever she went, the streets would be lined with cheering wellwishers. Never mind that the pavements were glistening with rain and that the water just poured down the backs of our necks, we were British and we had come to show the rest of the nation, especially those southern softies, that a spot of inconvenience would not prevent us from showing the flag.

Above: A Royal Variety Show at the Palace Theatre in 1959 saw Queen Elizabeth, the Queen Mother, gracing the occasion with her presence. That winning smile greeted the stars to whom she was presented just as it would for more than 40 years until her death at Easter 2002. Here was a woman as old as the 20th century, having been born on 4 August 1900 in Hertfordshire, though she spent much of her childhood at Glamis on Tayside. The Queen Mum, as she became affectionately known, was a highly respected and much loved royal. Here she was being introduced to one of the most glamorous stars of the 1950s. Liberace was a fine concert pianist who branched out into the world of variety, bringing to it a glitz that was years ahead of its time. With his candelabra atop of his piano and his outrageously sequinned costumes this American could command huge fees for his stage and television work. His schmaltzy talk about his mom and brother George made many cringe, but they still paid good money to see him. When criticised he said, 'I cried all the way to the bank'. He won damages from the Daily Mirror's gossip columnist Cassandra in June 1959 when it was implied that he was a homosexual. The flamboyant Wladziu Valentino Liberace died on 4 February 1987.

Above right: Even our parents grudgingly admitted that there was something likeable about the quartet of cheeky Liverpuddlians who took the mid 1960s by storm with their yeah, yeah, yeah and introduced the word Beatlemania into our language. Mum and dad might have winced at their mophead haircuts and some of the loud tunes they played, but they seemed like nice boys underneath. But, when it came to the Rolling Stones then that was a totally different matter. Much to their parents' disgust these young fans, seen in 1965 on Oxford Street, were ready to enter the Palace Theatre and scream their heads off in support of Mick, Brian, Keith, Bill and Charlie. The Stones were anathema to the older generation as they represented everything that was wrong with the youth of the day, in its opinion. They wore scruffy clothes, looked unkempt, wore their hair at a ridiculous length, played their music at an ear splitting level and were known to dabble in drugs. Teenagers loved them. In the theatre the Rolling Stones could have played any song they wished because the audience never heard a note as it was too busy screaming the house down.

Christmas was coming in 1958 and the band and choristers were out in force in Piccadilly Gardens providing a lunchtime concert for shoppers and office workers. Santa and his reindeer, in front of a Christmas tree backdrop, took a short rest from their busy schedule to listen to 'We three kings' or 'Away in a manger'. Those were the days when children carried lanterns and came round to our houses singing their carols and we invited them in for a mince pie and gave them a tanner for entertaining us. They do not come any more as their parents will not let them onto the streets at night and anyone asking a youngster to step across the threshold would be thought to have ulterior motives. Modern society has consigned such youthful innocence to the waste bin. Half a century ago children thrilled to the sight of a nurse's uniform or Dinky car in their stockings with a magic colouring book as an added extra. Now they demand and get designer clothes and the latest electronic gizmos. When did you last see a kiddie playing imaginatively by using the furniture as a fort for his toy soldiers or as a hospital for her dolls? When was the last time that the Salvation Army band came up your street and stopped on the corner to play 'Once in Royal David's City'?

At long last Matt Busby had achieved his dream and the European Cup could adorn the trophy cabinet at Old Trafford. A former Manchester City player, as United's new manager he had taken over a bomb wrecked ground and depleted team after the war. He took the first of his great sides to FA Cup triumph in 1948 and the League Championship in 1952, but then began to unravel the team as he developed the Busby Babes' policy of bringing in young talent. This wonderful set of young men won the title again in 1956 and were entered in the European Cup, a competition for champion clubs only. Despite objections from the dinosaurs in the Football Association, United swept all before them until they came up against the great Real Madrid, losing in the semi finals. Busby won the league title again in 1957 and his boys reached the European Cup semi final again, only to be cruelly struck down by the Munich air crash in 1958 that claimed the lives of eight players. During the 1960s another new side emerged, again reaching the European semi final in 1967 and going one better in 1968 when, at long last, that elusive trophy was lifted in a 4-1 defeat of Benfica. Busby and two survivors of the Munich disaster, Bobby Charlton and Bill Foulkes, shared a silent tear as the crowds cheered the arrival of the team for its civic reception at the Town Hall. They still sing Busby's name at United's matches today.

Shetlands. In Manchester it seemed that every street had its own wildly successful party, though cynics could be heard to say that we would never again see their like.

Left: During 1977 it appeared that the younger generation born in the late 1940s, many of them with young children of their own by then, had scant regard for the monarchy. Some of their attitudes towards the Royal Family rubbed off on their elders and it seemed as if the Queen's Silver Jubilee was going to be something of a damp squib. How odd that things changed so dramatically in the final few weeks leading up to the celebrations that marked the completion of 25 years of her reign. The official date of the anniversary was obviously that of her father's death and as it was hardly appropriate to hold parties to coincide with that, seven days in early June were designated as Silver Jubilee Week. From a slow start there was a sudden flurry of activity as the nation rediscovered patriotism. Bunting flew from lampposts and across roads, schools organised fancy dress competitions, memorial coins and mugs were dished out and people partied in the streets as old and young had a memorable knees up. Holywood Street, Moss Side had its tea party, tables and chairs were dragged out onto the pavement. and couples danced to Abba's 'Knowing me, Knowing you' and rounded off the session with loud choruses of 'Rule Britannia'.

Top: In 2002 how could we have doubted the support the country would show for Queen Elizabeth II's Golden Jubilee? The scenes of over 1,000,000 flag waving subjects cheering the procession on its way to Buckingham Palace warmed the heart of every true Brit. That it heralded England's defeat of Argentina in the World Cup and Lennox Lewis flattening Mike Tyson made it something even more special. The same reservations had been held 25 years earlier when we prepared to acknowledge a quarter of a century of duty. Yet, when the time came the streets were filled with happy, smiling faces all enjoying the special occasion and the festivities that accompanied it. Moss Side held a carnival and buses and lorries were commandeered for the day and turned into gaily decorated floats. A week of celebrations began on 7 June 1977 when a giant bonfire was lit in Windsor Great Park. As the flames illuminated the evening sky 100 other bonfires were lit by Lord Lieutenants, Mayors and Bishops from Land's End to the

On the home front

Below: It is incorrect to label these men as Withington Home Guard because they were still Local Defence Volunteers (LDV) in the spring of 1940. The woman with her children provided the only spectators to this marching band, but in the years to come thousands would turn out to acknowledge the role played by these volunteers and other members of the civil defence. At the end of the war the prime minister told the nation that the WVS, Red Cross, St John Ambulance, Land Army, ATS, Home Guard and the other various auxiliary groups formed the army that Hitler forgot. The men in this photograph were ready to stand firm if an invasion ever came and, in the meantime, lend a hand on other civil defence duties. The highly popular TV sitcom of the 1970s, 'Dad's Army', did these men little justice. Whilst it was very funny, it tended to belittle the work and dedication of these volunteers. It is true that in the LDV's early days there were instances of drills being carried out by men marching with broomsticks across their shoulders, but by the time they were renamed the Home Guard in July 1940 things had changed. Then this fine body of men, unarmed in this photograph, would be able to parade and practice with real weaponry, though, in truth, the range of equipment was still limited.

In the late 1930s we were slow to recognise that another major war was inevitable. Civil defence seemed to be a series of exercises for men playing at being soldiers and panicking unnecessarily. In 1937, when Fascist forces bombed the cultural and spiritual home of the Basques during the Spanish Civil War, it gave many of us an uneasy feeling. The destruction of Guernica was a mere foretaste of what was to come, but we were foolishly reassured by Prime Minister Chamberlain who returned from his meeting with Adolf Hitler in Munich in 1938 waving a piece of paper that promised 'peace in our time'. When the tanks rolled into Czechoslovakia a week later and Jews were beaten senseless on German city streets as their shops were looted during Kristallnacht we began to have second thoughts. Belatedly, air raid precautions were undertaken in earnest. Bomb shelters, like this one being opened by the mayor in tunnels under Chestergate, Stockport that held 4,000 people, were fitted out. Anderson shelters, named after the Home Secretary, appeared on waste land and in back gardens and gas masks were issued in an attempt to bolster our defences to attack. The Air Raid Wardens' service had been created in 1937 and the Women's Voluntary Service in 1938, but initial response to these and similar organisations was slow amongst the apathetic British. However, when reality dawned the civil defence units received a flood of volunteers.

When it came to civil defence Britain had to rely on a variety of ordinary people to take over duties that would normally have been the remit of hardened professionals. Air Raid Precautions (ARP) were handed over to civilians, some of whom were in reserved occupations but also included a large number who were too young, too old or the wrong gender to be called up into the armed forces. This member of Salford's ARP was a young woman willing to put her own life on the line in the interests of the country. She pedalled her bicycle furiously around the streets advising householders to observe the blackout, waving a rattle or blowing a whistle to warn of an air raid and remaining at her post as bombs exploded around her, waiting for an opportunity to go and assist the rescue teams. When our young people showed such courage and dedication it is little wonder that we pulled through, despite everything that Hitler chose to throw at us. The Duke of Kent must have been impressed with that steely look of determination she showed when being presented to him in 1941. He was the husband of Princess Marina of Greece and father of the present Duke, Princess Alexandra and Prince Michael. His life ended tragically in a flying accident the following year.

Above: High explosive does not differentiate between good and evil, it just destroys indiscriminately. To a bomb aimer flying high over the city this was just one more target in the attempt to cripple our industries and wreck our spirits. The Victoria Memorial Jewish Hospital could never have been classed as a legitimate subject for an aerial strike, but the bombs that fell did not care. They exploded without being able to separate factory from church or soldier from innocent child. This was not the only occasion when a hospital was hit because six months later, in June 1941, 14 nurses lost their lives when Salford Royal Hospital was hit. It must have been terrifying for nurses and patients as they tried to get to the bomb shelters. Some of the sick could just about manage to walk unaided, but others needed to be wheeled in chairs or in their beds. There were others too ill to be moved and the bravery of those heroines who stayed at their posts can never fully be rewarded. World War II was the first and, let us pray, the last time that civilians were involved in all out hostilities on an almost daily basis. It was not only industrial areas that became targets because Hitler extended the Luftwaffe brief to include towns that had a particular historical or cultural importance. Bath, York and Norwich all were hit in the Baedeker raids, so named after the guide book from which the Fuhrer selected his victims.

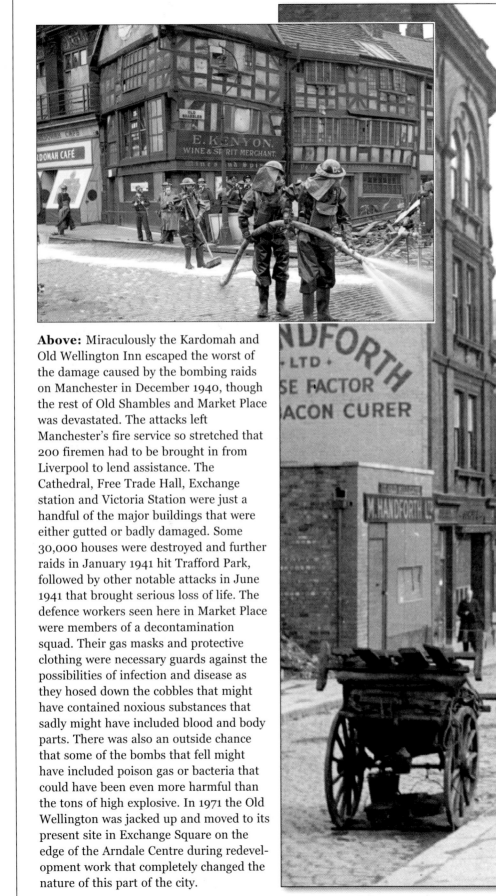

Above: Miraculously the Kardomah and Old Wellington Inn escaped the worst of the damage caused by the bombing raids on Manchester in December 1940, though the rest of Old Shambles and Market Place was devastated. The attacks left Manchester's fire service so stretched that 200 firemen had to be brought in from Liverpool to lend assistance. The Cathedral, Free Trade Hall, Exchange station and Victoria Station were just a handful of the major buildings that were either gutted or badly damaged. Some 30,000 houses were destroyed and further raids in January 1941 hit Trafford Park, followed by other notable attacks in June 1941 that brought serious loss of life. The defence workers seen here in Market Place were members of a decontamination squad. Their gas masks and protective clothing were necessary guards against the possibilities of infection and disease as they hosed down the cobbles that might have contained noxious substances that sadly might have included blood and body parts. There was also an outside chance that some of the bombs that fell might have included poison gas or bacteria that could have been even more harmful than the tons of high explosive. In 1971 the Old Wellington was jacked up and moved to its present site in Exchange Square on the edge of the Arndale Centre during redevelopment work that completely changed the nature of this part of the city.

The city centre was hammered by the aerial bombardments of the second world war. Trafford Park was a vital part of the country's war machine with its engineering and aircraft manufacturing plants, especially those of MetroVickers. The production of the Lancaster bomber and radar equipment and the large arsenal here, in addition to the nearby oil terminal, made Manchester a prime target for enemy action. A major assault was launched late in 1940 when, in the three nights leading up to Christmas, incendiaries and high explosive set the city on fire and reduced much of the centre to rubble. In the first night of the raids 233 bombs exploded during a five hour period of terror that destroyed or damaged nearly everything within a one mile radius of Albert Square. A huge proportion of Manchester's commercial and historic wealth was wiped off the map in that short space of time. The aftermath in Market Place showed the carnage that had been brought to this once attractive old quarter. The Corn Exchange was damaged, but still stood overlooking the piles of bricks and fallen masonry underneath the shadow of its dome. In 1903 it had replaced the previous 1837 building on Hanging Ditch at a cost of £350,000. Censorship rules meant that the bombing was initially reported as affecting a 'town in the northwest', but anyone living within 20 miles of the city could have identified it from the glow in the night sky.

The Crusader tank bowling along Princess Street in 1942 was part of a morale boosting and fund raising exercise for the war effort. It was a sight that impressed the large crowd that turned out to witness the event. Hardly a month seemed to pass by without some appeal being made to the nation's generosity. There was Warship Week, Spitfire Week and Wastepaper Week, all dedicated to the cause of encouraging us to give what we could to help win the war. Some remarkable feats of recycling took place as pots and pans, old railings and rusty nails reappeared above our heads as a fighter plane or set sail as a destroyer bound for the open seas. Some towns raised money to adopt their own tanks and thermometers were erected on town halls to chart the progress of cash flowing in to swell the coffers. Old curtains, rags and clothing were collected by the Women's Voluntary Service and were restyled as parachutes or uniforms. There seemed no end to the imagination of those in charge of scouring the country for anything that might be remotely useful. Britain became a land of hoarders as families never threw anything away for fear that they would be accused of being wasteful and all the time we turned our back gardens into mini allotments as we dug for victory.

Above: Although some buildings nearby escaped virtually unscathed there was no reprieve for the Free Trade Hall as it suffered a dreadful beating from the attacks from above on 23 December 1940. Edward Waters designed this famous Peter Street building and work on it began in 1853. Having cost £40,000 the official opening ceremony took place on 10 October 1856. Originally called Manchester Guild Hall, it had a seating capacity of 3,165 and was one of the city's major centres. It lay as but a shell for the rest of the war but was restored to its former glory and reopened by Queen Elizabeth in 1951 in one of the last public engagements she performed before being sadly widowed the following February. The Free Trade Hall has hosted a variety of events, ranging from religious meetings to wrestling and from exhibitions to school speech days. In the early 20th century suffragettes held rallies within its walls and a variety of political philosophies have been heard echoing from its stage over the intervening years. However, for most people the Free Trade Hall will forever be associated with the orchestra named for Charles HallÈ, the first principal of the Royal Manchester College of Music. Under the baton of John Barbirolli, conductor from 1943 to 1968, the HallÈ continued and perhaps surpassed the reputation built up during Hans Richter's time as its conductor at the start of the century. The orchestra is now based at the Bridgewater Hall.

Below: The big wigs were out in force in what was left of the Royal Exchange in early 1941. They had come to view the damage caused in the previous month's air raid. Included in the official party were the Home Secretary and King George VI, but it was Queen Elizabeth who was taking the lead as they viewed the wreckage of the third Royal Exchange in Manchester's history. This building was erected in 1874 and, after being enlarged, was reopened by George V in October

1921. During the war Queen Elizabeth was often at the forefront of such scenes as she guided her nervous husband through his royal duties. Born Elizabeth Bowes-Lyon in 1900, she had little expected to be thrust so far into the limelight, even when she married the Duke of York in 1923. When her brother-in-law, Edward VIII, abdicated in 1936 and her husband stepped into the breach, she helped him take the reins by involving herself as no previous consort had done before. The couple endeared themselves to the general public by refusing to slip away to a safe haven in Canada and stayed at home to brave the dangers of aerial bombardment just like the rest of us. This was supposed to be a secret visit, but word soon got out and before long wellwishers arrived to give the royal couple a rousing cheer.

Bottom: That some famous and historic buildings survived the air raids was just a matter of luck. The Midland Hotel, Town Hall, Central Library and Art Gallery somehow managed to avoid the fate that befell so many others that were reduced to burnt out shells or became just so many piles of rubble. The aftermath left a pall of acrid smoke and brick dust hanging over the city as though it were some sort of relation to the industrial smogs that bedevilled residents until the 1950s. Workmen sifting through the debris were surprised to see King George VI arrive for his own personal assessment of the damage. His visit had been kept as quiet as possible for security reasons, though it did not take long for word to spread that he had honoured Manchester with his presence. Quite what the bobby on the left was guarding is difficult to fathom as little of value had been left intact and, thankfully, we were not a nation of looters. We were more likely to salvage something on behalf of a neighbour than keep it for ourselves. Wartime was a horrid experience but there really was an atmosphere of bonding and togetherness in the struggle against a common foe. To see the King take an interest was a firm morale booster.

Streets of change

Above: Cobbled carriageways, tram tracks and black saloon cars heading down from Piccadilly take Portland Street back to 1935 when Europe was about to experience turmoil once more. Mussolini's Italian army set sail for Abyssinia and the German Chancellor, Adolf Hitler, provided a taste of what was to come by banning Aryan marriages to Jews and stating his intention to remove all Jews from public life. At home we seemed more concerned with the retirement of Jack Hobbs, England's greatest batsman, or Malcolm Campbell smashing the 300 mph land speed barrier in Bluebird. The League of Ovaltineys praising hot, milky bedtime drinks was more in our minds than warnings or warmongering put out by the League of Nations. There were also problems on our roads that occupied our minds. Compared with the number of vehicles that we had the road accident statistics were quite horrific. As can be seen here, pedestrians took their life in their hands as they braved the traffic to cross the street. Out in the suburbs or more rural areas things were just as bad. Little wonder that the 1930s brought in driving tests, Belisha pedestrian crossings, Percy Shaw's cats' eyes and more widespread electrically operated traffic lights. Road safety education came too late for one famous figure when TE Lawrence, of Arabia fame, was killed in a motor cycle crash in May that year.

Seen in 1939 from the station approach, Oxford Street's Palace Theatre had been in business for nearly half a century ever since it admitted its first paying customers during Whit week in 1891. It had originally been intended as a Palace of City Varieties but there had been a groundswell of Methodist mentality that objected to popular music hall and all that was associated with that style of entertainment. Influential figures railed against the culture of alcohol and dubious morality that seemed to accompany both the entertainers and their public, labelling all involved as drunks or degenerates or both. However a programme of grand ballet and similar artistic productions meant that the Palace could open without upsetting those who took the moral high ground, but for many years the theatre was denied a drinks licence. Once under way more middle of the road shows were put on and Little Tich, Dan Leno, Marie Lloyd and George Formby Senior all trod the Palace boards. Charlie Chaplin was on the bill in 1903 as the Palace went from strength to strength. By the middle of the last century it had gained a reputation for conventional drama, offering touring companies the opportunity to present productions. Many readers will also recall the fabulous pantomimes without which the Christmas season was not complete. The theatre closed in 1978 but reopened in 1981 after major refurbishment.

Nerves of steel, a steady hand, an eye for an angle and a head for heights are just a few of the qualities needed by a photographer. This one stood high on the Central Library roof in 1946 to look across St Peter's Square and along Oxford Street towards the Palace Theatre that stands on the corner of Whitworth Street. It was a time to start the process of restoring both buildings and shattered dreams. That would not be easy and we remembered how difficult life was after the previous conflict when jobs were scarce and the war debt that accrued bit into the economy. It was not as if the whole world was at peace again. There was terrorism in Palestine and religious rioting in India, but the most worrying development came to our notice when America tested an atomic bomb at Bikini atoll in the Pacific. At home there was a flourishing black market in nylons, chocolates, perfume and other scarce commodities. Crime was on the increase again and the man in the street was not as confident of a rosy future as he had been on VE Day. Then he had stood near the Cenotaph in St Peter's Square to celebrate the end of the war and remember those who had fallen. This memorial, designed by Lutyens and originally intended for Albert Square, was not consecrated until 1924, having been delayed by the withholding of royal assent for moving the Albert Memorial. The cross on the left marks the site of the altar of the old St Peter's church.

Right: The little railway bridge is alongside Oxford Road station as we look towards Oxford Street and the Palace Theatre. The Grade II listed Victorian terracotta Refuge Assurance buildings, now the Le Meridien Palace Hotel, are beyond the bridge on the right and the block that dominates the foreground now includes the HSBC bank amongst its other occupants. The photographer was standing opposite where the BBC TV studio can now be found, with Charles Street to the right. Traffic was light in 1950 and such a picture today would include a sea of traffic that included drivers entering the city centre about to be confused by the one way system as they looked at the various bans on turning one way or another. There is probably some poor motorist who has been driving around Princess Street, Whitworth Street, Oxford Street and Portland Street in ever decreasing circles for the last 12 months wondering if he is ever going to escape their clutches. Miss your turning and there is no time to correct the manoeuvre with impatient drivers honking their horns behind you. All that you can do is go round again and pray to get it right next time. In the middle of the last century there was time to look around and admire some of the impressive architecture, but those days are long gone even though the buildings in this photograph are still with us.

Below: Manchester Cathedral, seen in the distance, dates from a structure erected in the 15th century, though there had been places of worship there before. It was extensively renovated on several occasions in the 19th century and its 130 foot tower rebuilt in 1887. The new Lady Chapel was created during repairs needed after the cathedral was badly damaged by the 1940 bombing. Deansgate in 1950 was very quiet, but car ownership was not widespread and fuel was still in short supply. There must have been something very eyecatching in Vivian Grant's window as several heads have turned to have a good look. Above them was lettering promoting pianos and radios. It was still popular to have a piano in your drawing room, even if no one could play it properly, as it was a sign that the family came from a cultured and sophisticated background despite a lack of obvious wealth. Having a piano smacked of holidays at Lytham St Annes rather than Blackpool and suggested that tea was eaten using two knives and a fork, one of the knives being reserved for spreading butter on the bread. A radio was an essential piece of equipment for both information and entertainment. The Home programme brought the news and serious drama and the Light gave us 'Much Binding in the Marsh' and 'ITMA', though we rather drew the line at a turgid Mahler symphony on the Third programme.

Since opening in 1755 the Royal Infirmary was the main building in this area that was developed from what was once an old clay pit. After the hospital's closure in 1908 and subsequent demolition Piccadilly Gardens were developed as an idyllic green oasis in the centre of the city where the housing around about was being replaced by hotels and commercial buildings. The bus terminus was opened on the edge of Piccadilly and now serves modern trams as well. This open view of Piccadilly Gardens is one to savour as it has been affected by the craze for high rise structures over the last 40 years. Piccadilly Plaza, that concrete slab of a place, began to raise its contro-versial face well above the skyline in 1959 and it took until 1965 to complete the hotel and office blocks. The demand for building more and more developments continues into this century as the Argent Group remodels the area known as the Piccadilly Triangle. That will include an office block and car park on the gardens that will be remodelled, but can never again recapture the serenity of the scene that was photographed in 1953. Then they looked so pretty as decorations were prepared to celebrate the coronation of Queen Elizabeth II. As we got ready to enjoy the moment little did we know of the concrete shadow that was soon to fall across Piccadilly Gardens.

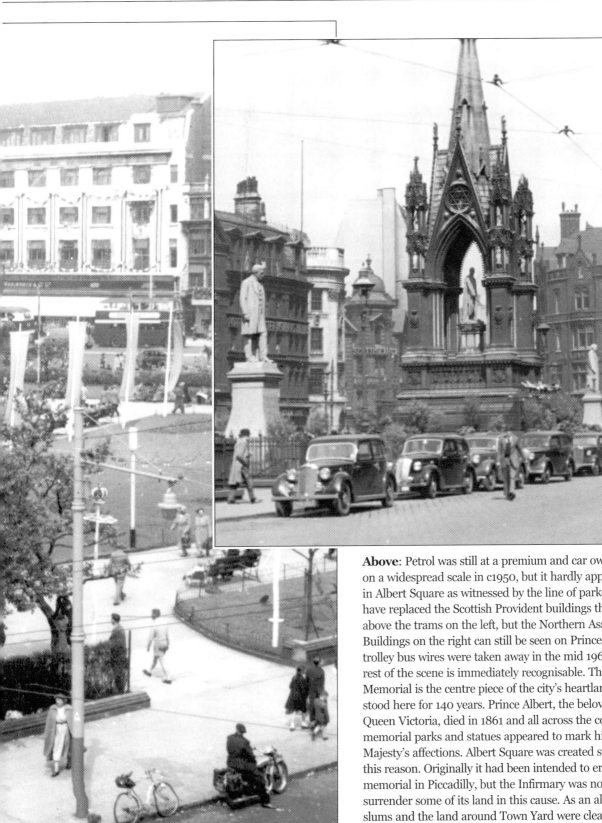

Above: Petrol was still at a premium and car ownership not on a widespread scale in c1950, but it hardly appeared to be so in Albert Square as witnessed by the line of parked cars. Shops have replaced the Scottish Provident buildings that towered above the trams on the left, but the Northern Assurance Buildings on the right can still be seen on Princess Street. The trolley bus wires were taken away in the mid 1960s, but the rest of the scene is immediately recognisable. The Albert Memorial is the centre piece of the city's heartland, having stood here for 140 years. Prince Albert, the beloved husband of Queen Victoria, died in 1861 and all across the country memorial parks and statues appeared to mark his place in Her Majesty's affections. Albert Square was created specifically for this reason. Originally it had been intended to erect a memorial in Piccadilly, but the Infirmary was not keen to surrender some of its land in this cause. As an alternative, slums and the land around Town Yard were cleared to provide space for the memorial and the creation of the new Town Hall. The previous centre of administration had been on King Street, but the accommodation was too small after Manchester became a city in 1853 and the demands upon local government increased.

Top: In 1958 the Clarendon Hotel on Oxford Road was still part of the culture largely dominated by mature males. Pubs were places where you could escape from work or the missus and enjoy a pint or two with pals and put the world to rights. Earnest conversations about the fortunes of United and City took place without any satisfactory conclusion ever being reached. The government of the day was pulled to pieces, but still returned to power in the next election. However, agreement was reached on the ridiculous state of youngsters' clothing and their noisy music. Drainpipe trousers, fluorescent socks and long sideburns were not what they had won a war for and that stupid Elvis Presley with his wiggling pelvis would never replace Perry Como or Bing Crosby, now would he? When the men met up again the following evening they had the same conversation over and over again, but never seemed to tire of it. The drinking revolution of young people with their Babychams, Watney's Red Barrel and 'do 'ave a Dubonnet' would come in the 1960s, driving the old timers further into the corners of their public bars to mutter darkly about what the world was coming to. They even let unaccompanied women into pubs. Now that was the last straw.

Above right: Were they the best days of our lives? The teachers at Manchester Central Grammar School for Girls on Whitworth Street would have had us think so, but we were too busy living life to the full to dwell on such prissy statements. Anyway, it was hardly memorable sitting in class in 1958 trying to take in what this Pythagoras chap had been on about with his squares, sides and something about a hypotenuse. We had enough to worry about with clausal analysis, trying to determine whether these words made up an adverbial or adjectival clause. What did we do with it when we discovered what it was and has anyone ever found a use in real life for finding out the length of a ladder leaning against a wall or the height of a tree from the shadow it cast upon the ground? We would have been better off learning how to get the same salary from our employers in the 1960s as the young men next to us were being paid for doing the self same job. Still, we can look back on lessons spent playing up to the male student teacher who thought he was God's gift to women, the times we went on field trips and smuggled a bottle of Martini into the dorm or that occasion we spotted the deputy head sitting just a little too close to the art teacher from the boys' grammar school one lunchtime in the Kardomah. Those were the best days.

If this cinema on Market Street is instantly recognisable then the likelihood is that you are male and own a grubby mac. The Cinephone stood next to Yates' Wine Lodge and, in 1957, would have been doing good business in X certificate movies. The film titles left little to the imagination and 'Nudes in the Snow' was almost what you got, but the censors of that era would not allow audiences to see all that they hoped for. The Cinephone, known to local wags as the Sin-e-phoney, was usually patronised in part by spotty boys of early teenage years who bought their entrance tickets in a falsely gruff voice hoping to convince the cashier that they were over 16. The remainder of the clientele consisted of middle aged 'saddos' who often entered the foyer with collar turned up, hat pulled down and copy of Reveillé rolled up in an inside pocket. It might be an interesting game to play if the reader looks closely at the pedestrians on the pavement and tries to determine which, if any, is likely to cross the cinema's threshold. It all seems silly and tame to us in the 21st century when the content of modern television programmes can be far more lurid than anything on offer in the Cinephone, but at the time the fare on offer was eye opening in every sense.

Above: Corporation Street was constructed in 1845, running from its corner here with Market Street out to the north towards Collyhurst. In 1958 buildings were being created to host new or extended businesses, either by renovating sites or finishing off the last of the regeneration work from the postwar years. Whilst all the work continued around it Burton's carried on its traditional trade as a men's outfitter. Meshe Minsky, a Lithuanian Jew, changed his name to Montague Burton when he came to Chesterfield in 1900. By 1910 he had opened four shops and as his empire grew he moved his headquarters to a large factory site in Leeds and from there and his Harrogate home by the 1930s he was opening an outlet in a new town on a monthly basis. There were many rivals in his line of business and Hepworth's, Weaver to Wearer, Dunn's and Fifty Shilling Tailors all had their supporters. Slogans helped catch the public's imagination, as with John Collier's 'the window to watch', but Burton's was 'the tailor of taste'. The cranes swinging above Burton's in 1958 returned with a vengeance

in the early 1970s when the Arndale Centre was begun. By the time of its completion in 1979 it had changed both the face and the shopping style of this part of the city. Over 200 shops were accommodated within its 30 acre site.

Inset: Poet Rupert Brooke was thinking of a vicarage in Grantchester when he asked 'Is there honey still for tea?' His romantic view of this land of ours was written nearly 50 years before this photograph of the Old Shambles in Market Place was taken in 1958, but the visions his words conjured up could have been applied to this little oasis of tradition. The building known as the Old Wellington Inn dates from at least as far back as 1550 and adopted its name as a pub in 1830. How popular a title that was in its early days is difficult to imagine since the Duke of Wellington, despite being a hero of Waterloo, was reviled in many quarters because of his association with the Peterloo massacre. Rupert Brooke's honey might have been available for serving in the Kardomah Café, a gentle haven for ladies of certain years to sip elegantly from their teacups whilst criticising the world around them. They tut-tutted about the drainpipe trousers and luminous socks worn by young men going past the window and despaired about the gyrations of

someone called Elvis who it seemed was rocking in a jailhouse. 'Pity they did not throw away the key,' one was heard to remark. Their tranquility was occasionally interrupted by a waitress shouting, 'Egg on a barm!' as she passed an order to the kitchen down a voice tube. Another branch of Kardomah was situated in St Ann's Square and is now a McDonald's, where they have never heard of poetry and, much less, Rupert Brooke.

Top: Zorro, the masked adventurer and righter of wrongs, was just one of the characters about whom we fantasised as children. Having seen a film in which he appeared we made cardboard shapes to which we attached a bit of elastic and wrapped them across our eyes. With a piece of wood doubling as a duelling sword, off we went slashing away madly at invisible opponents. On other occasions we came back home from the Saturday matinee full of excitement at the predicament in which Flash Gordon had been left in his latest cliffhanger when his rocket, trailing sparks behind it, had crashlanded on some remote planet and was left dangling over a precipice. We knew he would escape, but now had to be left until next week. By 1961 the Empress on Oldham Road, Miles Platting was beginning to show its age. Its earlier glories would eventually be lost to the dreaded scourge of bingo and stands now as a throwback to the days when this was a busy and thriving part of Manchester, with a large local population who lived and worked here. It opened in 1912 as the Empress Electric Theatre in the very early days of purpose-built cinemas. Its now somewhat forlorn facade of red Accrington brick harks back to the 19th century, giving it an industrial appearance but with almost castle-like cornice adornments to its pyramid shape. Used as a paint store in the early 21st century there are hopes that English Heritage can help save it as a listed building.

Above: The little lad leading the way across the Princess Street zebra crossing in 1961 will be about 50 by now. Can he remember what it was like to wear short trousers and have chapped legs in the winter time and permanent scabs on his knees from playground falls during a 25 a side game of soccer? Head down he was then thinking about the Biggles book that he had got out of the library and was anxious to lose himself in the WE Johns' plot of daring do, chocks away and camaraderie with Archie and Ginger. Tucked away under a cushion on the sofa was a copy of the Eagle with more adventure in the shape of Dan Dare, or perhaps he had other comics like the Hotspur, Rover or Wizard. Great stories awaited him when Limpalong Leslie overcame his handicap to score the winning goal, Alf Tupper ran along the track on a diet of faggots and peas and the mighty Wilson won the Ashes singlehandedly. It was grand to be a boy in 1961. There were seasons for conkers and marbles and girls to be teased. Dens were to be made out of old mattresses and bits of wood on the spare ground at the back of Auntie Muriel's house. She was not a real relative, but every child called a neighbour auntie or uncle 40 years ago.

Next door to the Café Royal on Peter Street the last film reels turned in the projection room of the Gaiety in June 1959 when the main feature, 'Al Capone', included a fine performance by Rod Steiger as the infamous Chicago gangster in this semi documentary style of movie. The cinema began life as the Gaiety Theatre of Varieties in 1878 on the site of an old circus. It burned down five years later and was rebuilt at a cost of £15,000 as the Comedy Theatre, reopening on 22 December 1884. It held 1,500 and was renamed the Gaiety Theatre in 1903 and prided itself on being something out of the ordinary, as instanced by some of the high admission charges. Even those in the wealthy middle classes blinked when asked for two guineas for the privilege of sitting in a private box. The Gaiety succumbed to the increased demand for picture palaces after World War I and made the switch from stage to screen in May 1921. There was some attempt to revive music hall and pantomime in the 1930s but with minimal success. The attractions of Hollywood were all too powerful and the record breaking 54 week run of 'Gone with the Wind' proved that audiences of the day had turned their back on old style entertainment. After the cinema's closure the site was cleared in August 1959 and Television House appeared in its stead.

Cobbled streets, back yards and terraced housing provided the backdrop for 'Coronation Street', the longrunning TV soap opera that was first screened in 1960, two years before these lads posed for the camera. The story lines in the early days typified life in the industrial north and concentrated on old dears like Ena, Martha and Minnie supping their milk stout in the snug. Women wore curlers under a headscarf and decorated their living rooms with flying ducks on the wall. The children played with whatever they could lay their hands on. These boys could have turned the cart into a chariot from the 'Ben Hur' movie they might have been lucky enough to see. On another day it would have been a stagecoach in which they rode with John Wayne, firing off imaginary six-shooters at outlaws or a covered wagon driven by Ward Bond's Seth Adams in 'Wagon Train'. In the latter case the lads imagined that it was part of a circle of such prairie schooners from which they could fight off an attack by Red Indians. Their private world was shattered when the window cleaner returned and told them to get off his cart, but then they had other things to which they could turn their attention. A battered old tennis ball, missing most of its outer fur, was produced and they had an enjoyable game of wall-y, kicking the ball against the brickwork as they honed the skills that might see Joe Armstrong or some other soccer scout give them the nod in years to come.

Right: In 1962 little children could play happily, whatever their surroundings. They are never more content than when messing about with old treasures that they have found. To them an old abandoned chair and a few other assorted bits and pieces can provide the basis for a den, something to call their own. Imaginations can run wild as they turn the most unlikely discoveries and inhospitable terrain into something in which they can lose themselves for a few hours, wrapped up in their own little world. If they came home at the end of the day with dirty faces and grubby knees then that was sure proof of the fun they had. These back yards and derelict sites in Hulme were gradually cleared as part of a slum clearance project and many of the families were rehoused in Wythenshawe or the other newly designated townships that developed in the suburbs to receive new populations. Hyde, Worsley, Heywood and the Langley estate in Middleton all received their share of new residents as 90,000 homes were demolished in a 20 year improvement programme that began in the mid 1950s. Tower blocks that appeared in Hulme proved to be socially disastrous and by the early 1990s many of these had been demolished to make way for a newer style of low level architecture.

Bottom: No look at Manchester would be complete without a visit to Coronation Street. The TV soap began in 1960 and is still near the top of the ratings over 40 years later. The film set near Granada studios has become one of the major tourist attractions in the city, but there are a number of real Coronation Streets in Manchester and some of them provided the inspiration for the original idea behind the successful programme. This one in Openshaw was photographed in 1964 and shows the typical terraced housing in which so many of us were brought up. There was a true sense of community and, although everyone knew each other's business, a real togetherness existed. Even so, mums were fiercely protective of their own families and even the best of friends could fall out if a child was the victim of some perceived injustice at the hands of another. They ruled the roost and dad tipped up his pay packet each week as his wife doled out money into tins for the rent man, electricity, Christmas club, shopping etc before giving him back his beer and baccy money. Each street had its own particular characters, the grumpy granddad, the flighty piece at number 19 or the stuck up lah-de-dah with net curtains and a son who had passed his 11 plus.

All in the best possible taste

Did you know that Manchester's GH Sheldon Wholesale Bakers Ltd bakes a 100 million baked products every year making Openshaw the Oven Bottom Muffin capital of the world? No? Well you do now.

Bread - the staff of life, a truly natural food. Where would we be without it to make sandwiches, to mop up our gravy or to make our breakfast toast? Bread has been known for thousands of years, baked by housewives, (or perhaps that should be cave-wives) since time immemorial. So important is the idea of bread and home that even the very word 'man' is ultimately derived from one of our ancient words for loaf.

Primitive ways of making bread can still be seen today in less developed parts of the world, with unleavened dough baked on flat heated stones. Who first learned to add yeast to dough in order to allow fermentation to take place and let the dough rise before baking is beyond recorded history - but the process was already well established in Mesopotamia and around the Mediterranean in classical times.

For housewives making bread has always been a hard if worthwhile task. How many husbands, coming home from the fields and forests ravenous with hunger, salivated as they sniffed the air as they detected the welcoming scent of newly baked bread waiting for them on their return.

No doubt thanks and appreciation were profuse; but that did not take the hard work out of the process. What housewives really

Above: Harold Sheldon as a young man.
Below: Harold's young assistant fuelling up at a customer's house in Failsworth.

war, but major changes in production capacity meant they would be progressively challenged by larger commercial bakeries operating on an industrial scale. And one firm which would keep pace with those changing trends was GH Sheldon Bakeries.

Today GH Sheldon Wholesale Bakers Ltd is a third generation family run business producing some of the most popular bread and bakery products in the country.

The company was established by Harold Sheldon in 1949 and within three decades was being run by his son Graham as Managing Director with his wife Barbara as Company Secretary. Their son Lee was by then also a director, so ensuring a continuing legacy of family pride and commitment. For over half a century the firm has been renowned for its high quality products at affordable prices, and an unwavering commitment to customer service.

From its very modest beginnings in a two roomed bakehouse-cum-shop in a Manchester back street the firm has successfully developed into a multi million pound business, now operating from a modern, purpose-built bakery from which it supplies many of the country's major supermarket chains and leading independent stores.

Best known for its unique signature product, the Lancashire Oven Bottom Muffin, the team of skilled and dedicated bakers at GH Sheldon also produces a wide range of fresh bread products. Using only the finest ingredients and baking to traditional recipes and processes developed down the generations the name of GH Sheldon has become synonymous with quality and value. Many of the products are made to secret family recipes which have been passed down though the generations - they each help the firm to deliver its promise - to put good taste into everyday life.

needed was someone else to do the job for them. That demand and the emergence of cities in the Near East led eventually to specialisation and the arrival of the professional baker. Fresh bread daily was the watchword of those early bakers, just as it is today. Bakers even then worked through the night baking bread so that it would be ready for sale first thing each morning. And, for those who still preferred their own recipes but could not be bothered to light a fire in order to do the baking themselves, bakers offered another service - bring your own dough and we'll bake your bread for you! Such a service persisted down the centuries and was still common in England until relatively recent times: and in some cases it was a wise precaution since - the adulteration of flour by any number of cheap substitutes such as chalk, straw, and dust by some unscrupulous bakers persisted far into the 19th century.

In Britain small corner shop bakers remained the dominating force in bread making until the second world

Top left: Harry Shields, early associate of Harold Sheldon. *Above left:* Uncle Bob Sheldon takes a well-earned breather. *Right:* One of Sheldon's early delivery vans.

In 1924 the young Harold Sheldon left school and began work as a baker for Horrock's Bakers in Goodier Street, Newton Heath, Manchester.

At Horrock's Harold learned the basics of the baking trade and also worked as a van boy on the delivery vans, helping on deliveries and in his spare time, when he was not on the road or baking, acting as stable boy to the horses which used to pull the bread vans. Harold could not have imagined where the world of baking would eventually take him despite being a capable and ambitious young man. Perhaps one thought did however occur to him: throughout the post war recession, and the great depression which followed the economic crash of 1929, people still needed to buy bread. Though thousands of firms went bankrupt and millions were on the dole, feeding the population remained a safe secure occupation. No matter how impoverished people might have become and be forced to do without luxuries no-one could do without bread. Yes life for Harold could have been very safe indeed had it not been for a certain Herr Hitler and his Nazis.

By the time the second world war broke out on 1939 Harold had progressed to become a delivery man with his own round, making door to door deliveries to his customers in the Failsworth, Chadderton and Oldham areas. Using a horse and cart certainly had some advantages over a modern van: Harold had no worries if ever he took time off and someone else took over his round - his horse was so experienced that it could travel the route without being told where to go.

Despite being in a protected occupation and therefore not subject to immediate call up Harold enlisted in the Royal Signals Regiment in 1939; he spent the next three years as a motor cycle despatch rider based in Salisbury where his wife Bertha and their daughter Audrey moved to be near him. After suffering serious injuries in a motor cycle accident however Harold was medically discharged from the Army in 1942 and

moved back home to Manchester.

That could easily have been the end of this story but Harold was made of stern stuff and after a lengthy recuperation period he rejoined Horrock's in his previous job. The work with Horrock's continued until 1949 when Harold decided to leave to set up his own bread and confectionery wholesaling business obtaining his products from the numerous independent bakers which still existed at that time.

Harold's drive and determination soon saw the business grow considerably; with help from his brother Bob and his brother-in-law Harry Shields, Harold saw his vans travelling as far as Huddersfield and Blackburn on a daily basis - despite the lack of a modern road network.

*Top right: Harold Sheldon. **Top left:** Harold's wife, Bertha. **Above right:** Barbara Sheldon's mum, Elsie - stalwart of the Topaz Street bakery. **Above:** 'Bertha' - Sheldon's vintage replica van - based on one of Harold's early delivery vehicles and named after Graham's mum.*

Another change of direction came in 1954 when H Sheldon Wholesale Bakers sold nine of its twelve vans as going concerns. This enabled the brothers to concentrate on providing the first class service that their customers had come to expect, whilst Harry Shields broke away from the firm after a short time and set up his own unrelated business.

Harold and Bob however worked together until 1964 when Harold entered into partnership with one of his former suppliers, Arthur Leigh, who had a bakery in Ashton Old Road in Manchester.

Leigh & Sheldon reduced the product range and specialised in the production of the now famous Lancashire Oven Bottom Muffins - they were soon counting many of Harold's former employees and almost every market in the district amongst their customers.

Larger premises were soon required and in 1967 the business moved to a new bakery on Clayton Lane, Openshaw. Harold's son Graham joined the business as a van man at that time to help sustain the growth that had already been achieved.

In 1969 another bakery was acquired in Dukinfield. Business continued to be successful and in 1971 Harold bought out Arthur Leigh's share of the partnership and sold the Dukinfield bakery as a going concern.

Sadly ill health now beset Harold, and in 1973 Graham acquired the business from his father. Graham ran the business with the

Above left: *Harold's son, Graham current Managing Director.*
Above right: *Graham's wife, Barbara, Company Secretary.*
Right: *Advertising poster from the 1980s.*
Below: *Baking at Topaz Street in the early 1970s.*

help of his wife Barbara and in 1975 moved to a brand new, purpose built bakery in Topaz Street, Beswick, Manchester. The new bakery was built on land that Graham had acquired from the local council a year earlier but much of it was later desired as part of the site of the Olympic 2000 bid by the City of Manchester.

GH Sheldon Wholesale bakers continued to invest and grow - a two storey extension was added to the bakery in 1977 and in 1988 the adjacent building was bought from the John Wallwork Volvo dealership to make possible a required production increase of around 70 per cent.

In 1992 however the City of Manchester announced that it was to bid to stage the Olympic Games of 2000. The Topaz Street site figured prominently as part of that bid and meant that the company had to move again. A new site in Stainburn Road, Openshaw, just a few hundred yards from Harold's former premises, was selected and building commenced in the Spring of 1994.

The new bakery, planned and designed by Graham, was fitted out with the latest state of the art equipment and opened in early Summer 1995.

Almost 70 per cent of the new plant and equipment was custom built to the firm's own design and specification. More than £2,5 million was invested in equipment alone, ensuring that its production facilities would be amongst the most modern in the country.

The move to the new bakery also provided the opportunity to significantly increase production in order to expand the business considerably and create new jobs enabling members of the local community to join the existing team. Over 70 staff were now employed, many of the firm's bakers having followed in the footsteps of their parents with the company.

Operating 24 hours a day, six days a week the bakery uses only the finest ingredients to ensure consistently high quality standards. Only the very best is good enough for GH Sheldon products whether it is the

Top left: A delivery van from the mid 1990s. Top right: Building work begins on the new site in Stainburn Road, Openshaw in 1994. Above left: Graham and Barbara Sheldon in front of the newly installed 50 tonne flour silo in 1995. Above right and left: The new, state of the art production facilities undergoing final checking.

3,000 tonnes of premium grade flour used in Muffin production or the succulent raisins and fresh spices in the firm's popular hot cross buns.

Production statistics have become truly staggering with more than 40 million muffins and 25 million potato cakes alone being produced annually.

A nine stage process begins with the mixing of the flour, liquid yeast and water into very large stainless steel bowls. It then moves on to 'make up', intermediate proving, which allows the dough to rise - pinning, where the dough is pressed into the required shape - panning, where the dough is positioned on baking trays - through to final proving and baking. After cooling the products are then boxed for delivery.

The firm now bakes over 100 million items every year, each as fresh as the last- and worth a massive £5

million at retail prices. Within a few years of having moved to the new bakery the firm could boast of having turned out enough muffins to stretch round the world one and a half times.

The company does not, however, rest on its laurels; it continues to look for ways to improve the service it gives to customers. It has now established a mobile Sales Support Team which is a familiar sight in their special fleet of distinctive vans. The team is able to respond rapidly to ensure that supplies to customers never run out whilst the fleet of 21 modern vans is a far cry from the horse and cart which Harold Sheldon had used to deliver the first bread he baked for customers so many years ago.

Today GH Sheldon is proud to be a company with a long history and a fine tradition. From its modest beginnings it has grown onto one of the leading independent, family owned bakers in the country, combining modern production facilities with an unswerving commitment to excellence in product and service to its customers all underpinned by values that have guided the business for over half a century. Openshaw looks set to remain the muffin capital of the world for a very long time to come.

Top right: Sarah Sheldon, successful barrister and future board member. **Left:** *Brand new bakery equipment - ready to "roll".* **Below left:** *Loading the firm's famous Lancashire Oven Bottom Muffins for delivery across the north.* **Below:** *Graham and Barbara's son, Lee, Company Director.*

With the sun on their backs two elegant ladies strolled around Boggart Hole Clough in the summer of 1935 as scores of others sat enjoying the fine weather and indulging in polite conversation. The baby in the pram was screened from the worst of the rays by a pretty canopy as her mother or nanny took the weight off her feet in this idyllic spot in north Manchester, several miles out from the city centre. It is the third largest park within the council boundaries and its valleys, cloughs and hills cover some 190 acres. The park is probably Manchester's most interesting leisure area as it balances the scenic delights of steep ravines and sloping gullies with the attractions of activities that include a boating lake, soccer pitches and an athletics track. An annual firework display is also very popular. Boggart Hole Clough is, in some ways, like Liverpool's Knotty Ash as many people think that they are fictitious place names. The comedian Ken Dodd confused many with his talk of Diddymen in Knotty Ash jam butty mines and a Radio Two disc jockey, the late Ray Moore, did the same with his references to Boggart Hole Clough on his early morning show. There are many tales about exactly what the word 'boggart' means, but most are centred around a ghostly spectre that haunted a farmer's family.

At leisure

Above: This is Whitworth Street's Ritz ballroom in 1930 where you could even hire a professional partner to help you enjoy an evening tripping the light fantastic. Until the beat groups came along and little dance clubs began to replace the large ballrooms, this was the face of dancing to popular music. There were crazes, just as in the 1960s when teenagers shook to the rhythm of the Twist, the Locomotion, the Funky Chicken and the Slosh, but between the wars they were the Black Bottom, the Charleston and the Lambeth Walk. But the most enduring steps were those danced to old ballroom favourites, the waltz, quickstep and foxtrot, with the more adventurous attempting the Latin American samba, rumba and cha-cha.

Learning to dance properly was a social necessity for being unable to take the floor was decidedly infra dig. Many learned to at Tommy Rogers' studio on Oxford Road or in one of the host of smaller establishments in the suburbs. Painter's still ran a flourishing business in Urmston long after the Beatles held sway. The music in the dance halls did not come from a DJ scratching away on a turntable but from live bands, usually with a lead singer up front. Many famous solo artists cut their eyeteeth in big bands under the leadership of Jack Hylton, Jack Payne, Harry Roy or Joe Loss. Some bands, though, kept their singers with them for years and Billy Cotton's show would not have seemed the same without Kathy Kay or Alan Breeze on vocals.

Above: Getting away from the hustle and bustle of Deansgate to spend a lunch hour near the river in Parsonage Gardens always has been a good idea on a nice sunny day. These office workers in 1950 were glad to take a break from pounding the heavy keys of their manual Remington or Underwood qwerty keyboards. Their work was punctuated by the ping of a bell as the typewriter carriage nearly reached the end of its journey, prompting the typist to hit the handle of the carriage return ready to start a new line. Accuracy was very important because there was no such thing as cut and paste or a delete key as we have on modern computers and word processors. Make an error and it was start again as the boss had no time for erasers and correction fluid. The office of half a century ago was one of carbon paper, bulldog clips, filing cabinets and card indexes. Then there were the shorthand pads on which to take down dictation in Pitman shorthand we had learned at night school. A walk in the gardens was a release from all this and conversation turned to plans for next Saturday. A night at the Ritz ballroom, dancing to the big band sounds and catching the eye of some chap still wearing his demob suit was very likely, but we had to be back home by 11.30 or dad would have had something to say.

The bowler hats of the bank managers in their business suits, the flat caps of the working classes, the utility hats of the housewives and the jauntily angled headgear of the pretty young things all came together to share a moment in the sunshine gleaming down upon Piccadilly Gardens. The man in uniform, strolling around the path, would soon be demobbed as his job was almost done in the summer of 1945. Little Jimmy could go to sleep in his own little room again, as Vera Lynn told us, now that the bombs had stopped falling and he felt safe once more. During the war there were air raid shelters on Piccadilly Gardens, erected to provide some protection for shoppers and workers when the sirens sounded as they often did. Wardens were in place to lend a hand with the organisation, keeping the shelters open from 8 am to 7 pm. The gardens have long been an attractive place to while away a lunch hour and just close your eyes and forget the ticking off that the boss has just dished out. In 1945 it was also an opportunity to reflect upon the debt we owed to the likes of the uniformed walker who had woken up each morning never knowing whether or not it was going to be his last.

Left: There is a carefree time in our lives that we wish we could bottle and take with us for evermore. When we were young and innocent the world was so simple, just a never ending round of fun and games. Pictured in Boggart Hole Clough in 1951 these swimsuited girls will now be dreaming of bus passes and retirement, but they will spare more than a passing thought for the days when they ran merrily through the shadows that dappled the ground under a clear, blue sky on that summer's day half a century ago. Rationing may have meant that the butter on their sandwiches was thinly spread and the meat portions were meagre, but they were free spirits and that was worth all the coupons in their mother's handbag. The young boy enjoying the shade of the tree was a product of the baby boom postwar years when families were reunited after

years of enforced separation and nature took its course. The stork put in for time and a half as the birth rate rocketed and Farley's sold out of rusks. Perhaps the girls skipping down the hill were rushing to tell their mother that they had really seen a boggart, that mischievous sprite renowned for playing impish pranks, though the true little imps are held captured forever in the centre of the camera lens.

Above left: School trips in a chara or double decker bus were difficult to arrange for Wythenshawe pupils in 1948 because fuel and spare cash were both at a premium. Fortunately, the local park was almost as enjoyable for a day out as taking a trip further afield. The teachers packed up crates full of beanbags, skipping ropes, rubber quoits and tennis balls so that relay races could be organised. There were games of leap frog and tunnel ball to be played and some of the lads brought their cricket bats along. Jack and Eric dampened their hair and slicked it back in the style of Denis Compton, the original

Brylcreem boy who the summer before had notched up over 3,000 runs for Middlesex. Sheila and Jane made daisy chains and wore them as necklaces as they strutted coquettishly like Rita Hayworth in 'The Lady from Shanghai'. One of the staff lolled against the tree, happily puffing on a Craven A without any fear that he was being a bad influence on his charges. They all enjoyed the break from times tables, spelling tests and handwriting practice as they relaxed in the 250 acres donated in 1926 by Lord and Lady Simon. Wythenshawe Hall, dating from 1540, was one of the park's main features and a former home to the Tatton family. It underwent major alterations in the 19th century and now houses an interesting art collection.

Above: Slightly reminiscent of a scene from Arthur Ransome's 'Swallows and Amazons' these happy boaters enjoyed the fun of the lake at Heaton Park in 1949. Out on the waters they could imagine that they were sailing off on some adventure or were taking part in a mini University Boat Race. The park is a wonderful place in which to spend the day as there is so much variety and space. When Pope John-Paul II said Mass here in 1982 over 1,000,000 were in the congregation. There are some ten listed buildings to enjoy, including the magnificent Heaton Hall, built in 1777 by James Wyatt for Sir Thomas Egerton. Combined with the pretty orangery, the Hall has become a popular place for wedding ceremonies. Kiddies love the farm centre and being able to see the animals at close quarters and there is plenty of room in the 640 acres of parkland for horticultural gardens, pitch and putt and an 18 hole golf course. Just as they did over 50 years ago families still come to picnic and play large family games of cricket on the grass, just as older generations did before them. In the year that this photograph was taken we reached the end of half a century that had brought us huge changes in transport on land and in the air, the arrival of mass communications via radio and television and the invention of miraculous vaccines and medicines that would extend our lives. It also brought the deaths of millions in two world wars.

Visitors to Belle Vue who wanted some excitement could go to the Wall of Death and watch motorcyclists defying gravity as they roared around the steep concrete wall. When the children arrived home that evening they got out their pushbikes and tried to emulate what they had seen by pedalling as fast as possible along some grassy bank on one of the bomb sites at the end of the street. It was no good, they always fell off. But they could not recreate the fun of an elephant ride. Children took the scenic railway ride, watched the chimps having their tea and then joined the jungle express, swaying in their perches as the great beast lumbered around the gardens. There were always long queues by the platform from which the riders got on board, but as about a dozen took the ride at any one go the waiting time was acceptable and well worth it. Phil Fernandez was in charge of the elephant rides. He was a popular figure, dressed in the eastern robes of his Malayan homeland. Phil brought his elephant Lil to Belle Vue in 1926 and after her death in 1947 promoted Annie, the animal in this 1949 picture, who had been bought from a circus in 1941. Phil continued to be a fixture at Belle Vue until his death in 1956.

Below: When Coronation Street arrived on Granada's TV schedules in 1960 it included a trio of characters who might have been modelled on the three women seen feeding the giraffes at Belle Vue Zoo in 1953. Ena, Minnie and Martha were representative of the bedrock of northern working class society, firm in their views and distrustful of change. As friends they were allowed to score points off each other, but fiercely defended one another's territory if ever it were threatened. The women with the keeper ruled their families with a rod of iron and won our respect for the consistency of their views and their behaviour. The schoolboy on the left, smartly dressed in his cap and blazer, would not have dreamed of doing anything other than wait his turn. Children knew their place and it was in the queue behind these pillars of society. The zoological gardens had long been a fixture, dating back to when John Jennison acquired the land in 1836. His small zoo grew with more land acquisition until, by Edwardian times, it occupied 69 acres behind its walls with a further 97 acres beyond. By then Belle Vue had become a huge entertainment complex with themed cafés and bars with three entrances being served from four railway stations. The zoo closed in 1967 and a major chapter in the Manchester leisure story came to an end.

Above: At first glance this might appear to be a scene taken from the leafy lanes of Cheshire or some quiet suburban spot on the edge of the countryside, so it may come as a surprise to realise that in 1957 these prams were being pushed in grounds within the closest of Manchester's parks to the city centre. The prams look dated as modern mums now wheel their offspring in sleek multi purpose vehicles that can be converted into pushchairs and car seats. Whitworth Park's 18 acres are situated on Oxford Road and were presented to the council in 1905 by the trustees of the estate of Sir Joseph Whitworth, the celebrated engineer and philanthropist. Born in Stockport in 1803, Whitworth developed a keen interest in the machinery of the industrial revolution and set up a precision engineering company in Chortlton Street in 1833. This was to be the forerunner of his great Whitworth works in Openshaw where he revolutionised accuracy levels from the accepted one sixteenth of an inch to a remarkable one thousandth. The Whitworth screw thread was the norm until metrication in the 1970s. Whitworth Art Gallery, now owned by the University of Manchester, is situated within the park and has a fine collection of wallpapers and textiles in addition to its paintings by Lowry, Hockney and other artists.

The woodland and open green spaces in Wythenshawe Park made for a delightful backdrop to the sandpits and paddling pool where these children splashed around without a care in the world in 1955. They hitched up their skirts and rushed happily in and out of the water before racing off for a game of hide and seek amongst the trees. Further over a budding Max Faulkner or Peter Alliss practised his golf swing on the pitch and putt course before joining the rest of the family for potted meat sandwiches and a bottle of Vimto. There were still those who had to keep a tight hold on their purse strings, but better times were just around the corner. The children were the product of the baby boomer years when men coming home from the war were reunited with wives and sweethearts from whom they had been separated for long stretches. Doing what came naturally saw the birthrate rise dramatically. There were more babies born in 1947 than in any year since 1921, itself a boom year after the first world war. One pleasing improvement came in the level of infant mortality when it fell to an all time low. The naive joy these children showed when playing on the swings and dipping their toes in the pool is something that parents cherished because a decade earlier they had not been sure if such happiness would touch their lives again.

John Jennison, the founder of Belle Vue Gardens, died in 1869, but his family continued the enterprise that eventually grew to become one of the major leisure attractions in the whole of the country. Rail connections and huge parking lots for cars and charabancs meant that access was excellent. Dance halls, dining suites, concert and sports halls, ice skating rinks, the zoo, speedway, a circus and funfairs were just some of the facilities that must have attracted millions of visitors through the turnstiles in the 20th century in the sure knowledge that they were guaranteed a great day out. Belle Vue enjoyed a huge boom after World War II as the nation demanded a lift for their lives in the austere recovery days of the 1950s. The Bobs and the Caterpillar were amongst the best patronised of the many attractions in the funfair. 'Bobbing' up and down on a roller coaster ride as girls screamed with a mixture of joy and fright may seem tame to modern youth, but in 1957 it was one of the scariest sensations around. For a quieter moment couples could cuddle under the Caterpillar canopy, safe in the knowledge that mum could not see what they were up to. She had a good idea, though, because she had taken that same ride with dad 20 years earlier.

Above: Manchester's Opera House is one of the best known theatres outside the West End, often putting on major productions by prestigious companies. In 1968 it was the turn of the Festival Ballet Company to delight us with its performance of Tchaikovsky's 'Sleeping Beauty', one of the most wonderful of ballets that has been graced by all the greats from Nijinsky to Nureyev and Pavlova to Fonteyn. The original intent for the Opera House, or New Theatre as it began life in 1912, was to provide Manchester with a new Shakespearean theatre and centre for grand opera. Designed by Farquharson, Richardson and Gill and holding 3,000 people paying from sixpence to five shillings, the Quay Street building was to undergo several changes of name in quick succession. In 1915 it became the New Queen's

Theatre and two years later the New Queen's Theatre and Opera House, before settling on its present title in 1920. In the 1940s and 1950s the audiences packed in to see such musical extravaganzas as 'Oklahoma', 'The King and I' and 'West Side Story'. Theatre going declined in the following two decades to the degree that the Opera House closed in 1979, briefly becoming a Mecca bingo hall. Thankfully it was restored to its true place in entertainment when it reopened under the Palace Theatre's ownership in 1984.

Top: By 1967 the Rialto on Bury New Road, Higher Broughton had become part of the ABC network of cinemas. The film 'Zulu', starring Michael Caine and Stanley Baker, had taken its time to arrive as it had been filmed in 1964. The adjacent buildings housed the Riverboat Club and Whisky a Gogo, illustrating the changing fashions in entertainment that in the late 60s and 70s spawned a mixture of establishments offering dance music and live acts. As time went on Wythenshawe's Golden Garter, Chorlton's Princess Club, North Manchester's Embassy and similar venues played host to the revival tours of acts whose stars had waned. They also provided openings for comics to make a name for themselves and a number progressed to national fame for a while via television's 'The Comedians'. Mike Burton, Ken Goodwin, Duggie Brown, Charlie Williams and George Roper were just some of the men for whom stardom came after years on the northern club circuit. 'The Wheeltappers and Shunters' Club', an amusing parody on working men's clubs, was also popular on the box.

Bird's eye view

This scene was captured looking along Deansgate, to the right, as it leads to Victoria Street where the cathedral and Chetham's School are situated. In the centre the Irwell heads the same way before almost joining them at Exchange Station. Dr Beeching had not reared his ugly head in 1959 and the days of his cuts were still a few years away. On the face of it most of his reforms were aimed at rural lines and stations, but they had their knock on effect in the city as services were rescheduled. Going back in time to 1830 when the first passenger service was established, it seems strange that it should be between Manchester and Liverpool, linking those two arch rivals in everything from commerce to pop music. Of course, by 1841 there were more than 1,300 miles of track in Britain and the nature of our lives changed as the population became so much more mobile as it found it easier to move around the country in search of employment.

In 1849 Exchange Station became the fourth to open in Manchester, though it was as much an add-on to Victoria Station as anything else. Victoria had opened on Hunt's Bank in 1844 and when the Exchange, named for the nearby Cotton Exchange, was built the continued platform with Victoria measured 2,194 feet, the longest in Britain. Exchange Station was demolished in 1969 and became a car park.

Barton Power Station was pumping out its fumes in 1958 on the Davyhulme side of the Manchester Ship Canal, across the way from Eccles and its famous currant cakes. The Victorian age was a time when rail travel and haulage expanded rapidly, so it was odd to see a new canal being built in 1887. There was good reason, for Manchester had come to depend upon Liverpool's powerful position. Allied with the port charges were high rail tariffs for moving freight and it was apparent good sense to try to counter the cost by seeking alternatives. Manchester was able to develop its own niche as a port and do away with the rail costs by opening the Ship Canal in 1894. The new artery also helped boost engineering in Trafford Park. It was a marvel of Victorian technology as the canal included an aqueduct across its width that carried the Bridgewater Canal. Barton Road swing bridge was another example of fine engineering, though lengthy traffic jams built up here in the days before the motorway bridge was built in the mid 1960s. Until about then rowing boats were still being sculled across the canal at the penny ferry in Irlam. The swing bridge was very useful to pupils at Salford's De La Salle Grammar School as it provided them with a good excuse for being late in a morning, though headmaster Brother Columba had heard it all before. Old Barton Road, the little lane meandering towards the top of the photograph, is heading almost towards the Trafford Centre shopping complex.

Sporting life

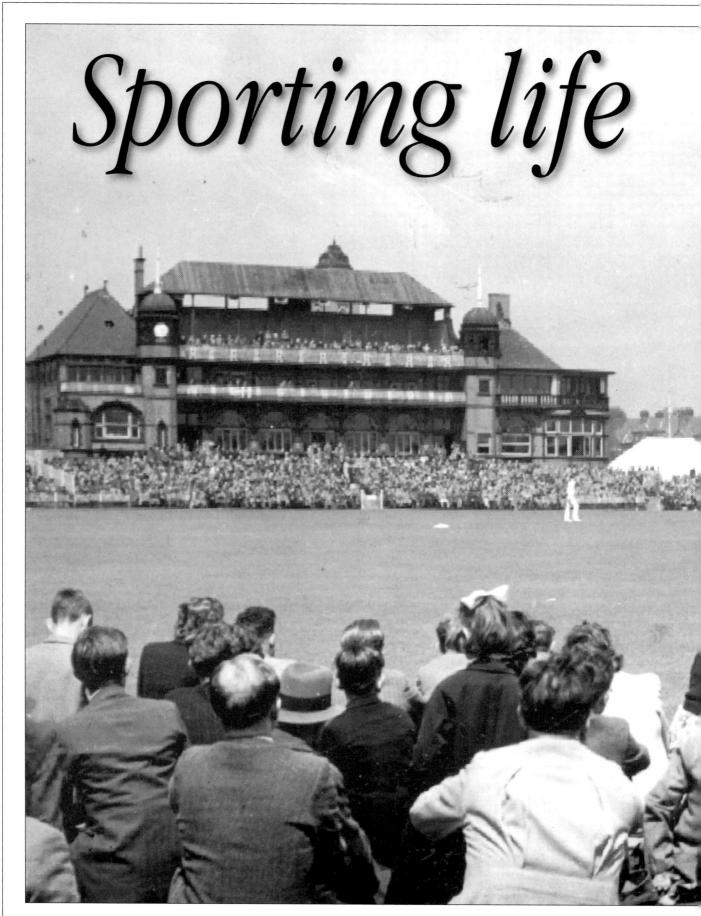

The sound of willow on leather under a balmy, blue sky brought crowds in their thousands to Old Trafford after the second world war. Starved of top class professional sport for so many years the public filled soccer grounds, speedway stadiums and cricket arenas week after week. This game in 1950 had seen people queuing down Talbot Road long before the umpires rang the warning bell that they were about to take to the field. The seats were filled and spectators spilled onto the grass inside the boundary ropes, craning their necks to get a glimpse of Cyril Washbrook and Winston Place about to set off on another opening partnership. It was the start of a fine decade of county championship cricket for Lancashire and it had some fine players who graced the scene. Geoff Edrich, one of a dynasty of excellent batsmen, was a cultured strokemaker and his efforts were well supported by Jack Ikin and the gritty Ken Grieves, whose slip catching ability was helped by his winter employment as a professional goalkeeper. Bob Berry, Roy Tattersall and Malcolm Hilton provided the slow bowling, but it was the speed and accuracy of quickie Brian Statham that wreaked the greatest havoc. Despite all these top players Lancashire could never quite match Surrey, the dominant force in the 1950s that won 7 championships.

Supporting Manchester City has always been something of a roller coaster ride, at one time hitting the dizzy heights and on others plummeting to earth in despair. Despite those ups and downs the club has retained a faithful local level of support that is the envy of many others. This 1955 match at Maine Road against Arsenal came during one of those periods of success when City could rightly claim to be on a par with their arch enemies from Old Trafford. That year Wembley beckoned and the team's defeat by Newcastle in the FA Cup Final was heavily influenced by a nasty injury to fullback Jimmy Meadows, reducing the side to ten men in those days when substitutes were not allowed.

True to their promise, the players returned to the twin towers 12 months later to defeat Birmingham in a match made even more memorable by another example of the Wembley injury hoodoo. City's keeper, the German Bert Trautmann, broke his neck during the game, but bravely played on. He did not realise how badly he was hurt until after the final whistle. The 1950s were wonderful times for soccer supporters who could enjoy cheering on their teams and swapping banter with visiting supporters without the worry of being beaten up by shaven headed thugs who began to ruin the beautiful game in the 1970s. Joe Hayes, Billy Spurdle, Bill Leivers and Roy Paul were the stuff that soccer was made of.

Below: Old Trafford has long been one of the country's major Test centres and was the scene for a remarkable feat of spin bowling by Jim Laker when he dismissed 19 Australian batsmen in the 1956 Ashes match. Quiz buffs will know who took the only other wicket. The following year it was the turn of India to pit its wits against a side that was about the best in the world and oh how we wish we could say that today. In the 1950s only Australia and the West Indies could run us close, with some modest claims being made by South Africa on occasions. India was only so much cannon fodder, especially in English conditions. The fire power of a permutation from Trueman, Tyson, Statham and Loader often blasted away a brittle batting order before the spinners got a chance to have their say. Despite many contests being one sided the attraction of Test cricket brought in the crowds who hired little cushions for a tanner to ease their aching bottoms for a vigil lasting seven hours or more. Schoolboys bought scorecards for threepence or brought with them their own scorebooks in which they carefully recorded every dot ball, wicket taken and run scored. At the end of an innings mathematical skills learned in the classroom helped them calculate each player's bowling average to two decimal places. By the way, if you are not a cricket buff then it was Tony Lock who took that other wicket, but anyone who was just 10 years old back then knows that.

Above: The grunt and grapple merchants at Belle Vue's King's Hall were a hugely popular attraction that packed the venue for over 25 years after the war. It was far removed from the modern American WWF style of ridiculously staged violence, mayhem and 'in your face' posturing. British professional wrestling was a mixture of skill and humour that crowds appreciated in equal measure. We all knew that most of the fights were rigged, but they were done with such panache that it was almost an art form. Whilst it was true that some little old ladies got carried away and rushed the ring trying to thump some protagonist with an umbrella, most of us sat back and joined in the fun by cheering the good guy and booing the villain. It was something like a pantomime performed on canvas. There were great families of wrestlers like Harry, Jackie and Bully Pye, refereed with increasing frustration by such as Dick the Dormouse. There were characters a-plenty with Masambula, the Simba Kid and Bert Royal. Who ever would have thought that Big Daddy was really Shirley Crabtree and that he lived in a little rural village in West Yorkshire? However, some of us guessed that Kurt Nielsen, despite his Viking helmet, actually turned a lathe by day at Mitchell and Shackleton in Patricroft and that his real name was much more mundane. The wrestling at King's Hall could always be guaranteed to finish at 10 pm so that the audience could get to the local in time for last orders. If the final bout began at 9.55 you knew a first round knockout was a certainty.

Heaton Park is the largest municipal park in Europe. The former estate of the Earls of Wilton has been owned by Manchester City Council since 1902 and represents 25 per cent of the green space in Manchester. In this 1948 still shot the mill chimneys in the distance remind us of the cotton trade that was so important to Lancashire, but was about to go into terminal decline. They were also partly responsible for the continual haze that hung over the city, turning to choking smog in the late autumn and winter months. People clutched hankies to the mouths or made little masks out of strips of material held on by pieces of elastic.

The various Clean Air Acts of the 1950s helped improve the environment to a degree we had never imagined possible. These men's shirts were grimy with specks of soot and dirt that hung around in the atmosphere. They took that for granted as they carefully balanced the virtues of thumb or finger bias, sending their woods skidding across the turf in a geometric arc. The 2002 Commonwealth Games used Heaton Park's four greens for its bowls competition and the standard was a far cry from old man's marbles as youngsters once dubbed the game. The park is listed as Grade II on English Heritage's register of historic parks and gardens.

Around the shops

Top: Paulden's, at the top of Market Street as it enters Piccadilly, became Debenham's, but it had flourished long before then on Stretford Road. This shot of the mighty department store was taken in 1925, by which time it had been established for nearly 50 years, and the company went on to give the city a century of service. Those of us who were brought up in and around Manchester will have their own fond memories of shopping here. We also remember the tricks that our mothers got up to. Five or six weeks before the Whit Friday Walks, known as Scholars' Walks, mums would head off on the bus on a journey of espionage. They carefully scrutinised and mentally recorded the patterns of the new season's dresses exhibited in Paulden's display windows and, using practised skills, ran up close copies and cut down versions for their daughters to wear in the Whit procession. When it came time for a new school uniform mum continued to show that typical Mancunian blend of thrift and nous. Henry Barrie's in St. Anne's Square was the official supplier of school uniforms but this monopoly meant that the clothing was pricey. You had to have the official tie, but it made more sense to buy a badge from Barrie's and sew it onto the right colour of blazer bought at Paulden's, Lewis's or Affleck and Brown for half the price.

Above right: It seems to be something of a waste of resources to have a policeman on point duty when all that can be seen for him to direct amounts to one horse and cart and a bicycle far off in the distance. On 7 June 1940 people had left their

cars at home, restricted as they were to a few miles of personal motoring each week. They went back to forms of transport that had served them well before the days of the internal combustion engine and that included using Shanks's pony as the woman on the right was doing. This generation thought nothing of walking miles and would be horrified to see 21st century mums in 4x4 cars and people carriers driving their children 200 yards to school. The building behind the bobby had contained a swimming pool, as can be determined from the lettering and the raised relief of a diver on the facade of the top storey. Manchester's archives record this photograph as showing the junction with Bridge Street, but there are arguments to place the scene further down the road at Quay Street. Whatever the location there was a job for the constable to perform, but as it was quiet he could have been forgiven for letting his mind wander as he recalled Churchill's stirring words, 'We shall defend our island whatever the cost may be,' uttered three days before.

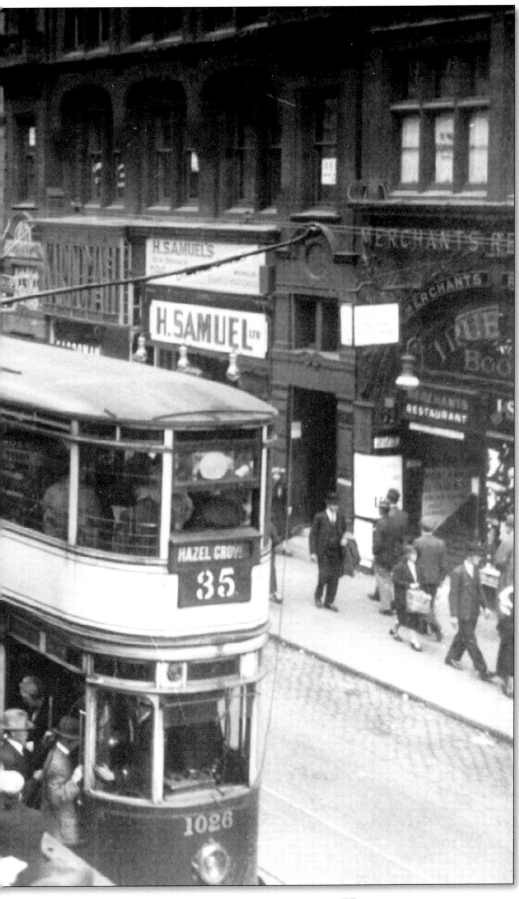

Market Street adopted its present name in the early 1800s and by 1939 had long been established as one of the main shopping areas of the city. Here we are looking towards Piccadilly with Lewis's on the right, a famous name that disappeared only in recent years. That department store was a favourite meeting place on a Saturday night for lovers who had travelled separately into Manchester and disembarked from their transport at the nearby bus station. Unfortunately, there were one or two ladies of dubious reputation who used to frequent the area, but the police kept a careful eye on them and usually moved them into Tib Street to book them as it was easier to spell than Piccadilly. The horse and cart at the bottom of the photograph remind us of the bygone age when rag and bone men came round the streets offering a donkey stone for the front step in exchange for whatever odds and ends we wished to throw out. The noble horse was once seen in great numbers on Manchester's streets, helping to provide public transport. The forerunner to this Hazel Grove tram, the horse drawn variety, operated until the end of Victoria's reign. Manchester Carriage Company, formed in 1865, eventually owned 385 trams and 3,583 horses. As each animal produced four tons of manure each year it was good news for rhubarb and roses.

Below: Looking along Market Street in 1957 the no waiting signs were the first attempts made to relieve congestion along this favourite shopping area. It is now pedestrianised and some of its shops now suffer from the fast food syndrome as the previous tenants moved into the Arndale Centre or on elsewhere. The man walking towards Preston's jewellers passed another looking into the window at Direct Raincoat, an establishment that promised it could undercut some of the bigger tailoring names. By the time the 1960s came along many traditional outfitters found it difficult to survive as jeans and T-shirts became the fashion and bright boutiques clamoured for the custom of that new consumer force, the teenager. Timpson's shoes had to battle hard for business against Tru-form, Saxone and Dolcis in a cut-throat business world. In 1957 it was stiletto heels on which young women tottered, much to the concern of the medical profession who felt that their feet would be deformed. Dance hall owners were not too thrilled either when they found pockmarked floors after an evening session. Young men also tested the doctors' nerves with their choice of footwear. Winklepickers with tapering tips cramped the feet quite painfully, but the lads about town did not care as they were the perfect complement to their luminous socks.

Right: Hope Brothers and Horne's are in this photograph, but the building on the right takes the eye. Marks and Spencer has moved around the Market Street area over the years, partly because of economic restructuring but also of necessity after the IRA bombing of 1996. In 1955 it was attracting its usual large share of custom to the store that opened in November 1931. Its original area of 18,000 square feet would be extended as business grew and the name became synonymous with quality and keen pricing. The company dominated the middle ground, particularly in the clothing trade, but its reputation became tarnished in the 1990s when accusations of drabness and fuddy-duddy styling were levelled at its products. However, the business seemed to have turned the corner and was attracting plaudits once more early into the new millennium. In a 2002 poll of things that were typically British Marks and Spencer was included high on the list with the monarchy, cricket and conversations about the weather. Michael Marks, 'don't ask the price it's a penny', began running bazaars before joining forces with Thomas Spencer in 1894. By the 1930s Marks and Sparks, as it affectionately became known, was established on many town centre streets. It can even argue that St Michael is the patron saint of underwear. Rows of skirts, jumpers and blouses sit alongside the children's wear. Many is the time you have been kitted out for the new school year in a Marks & Spencer grey shirt, blue jersey and pleated skirt. Well, you would have been if you were a girl, but who knows these days?

Alexandra Road runs south of the city, parallel to Princess Road, through Moss Side, the district that officially became part of Manchester in 1904. By 1960, when this warmly clad shopper was examining the hardware on the pavement, the population of the area had changed during the postwar period. In the late 1940s and 1950s Commonwealth countries were encouraged to supply labour for the British workplace. Factory hands, transport employees and nurses were targeted and many settled in places where they could identify more readily with their neighbours. In the early 20th century there was an influx of Jewish refugees fleeing persecution and they were concentrated in Didsbury and around Prestwich. In the second half of the century Commonwealth Asian families came to Longsight and Chinese settled in the city centre. Moss Side housed most of the West Indian population and along with the other ethnic minorities helped to provide a greater variety of life and culture into modern Manchester. As well as finding pots and pans for sale from pavement displays, shoppers came across yams, mangoes, sarongs and saris as bhangra, calypso and ska music drifted through the air. The aroma of fish and chips blends well with rogan josh, sweet and sour pork and pan fried chicken.

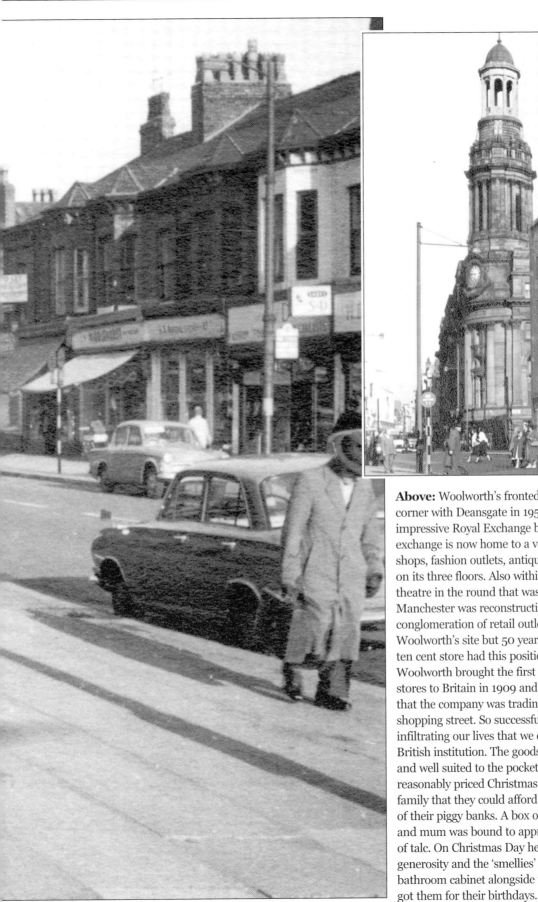

Above: Woolworth's fronted St Mary's Gate on the corner with Deansgate in 1955 under the shadow of the impressive Royal Exchange building. The old cotton exchange is now home to a variety of gift and specialist shops, fashion outlets, antique dealers and restaurants on its three floors. Also within its walls we can find the theatre in the round that was created at the time when Manchester was reconstructing its city centre. A conglomeration of retail outlets now trade from the Woolworth's site but 50 years ago the original five and ten cent store had this position to itself. Frank Winfield Woolworth brought the first of his American chain stores to Britain in 1909 and by the 1930s it seemed that the company was trading on every town's main shopping street. So successful did they become at infiltrating our lives that we came to regard them as a British institution. The goods were cheap and cheerful and well suited to the pockets of youngsters stuck for a reasonably priced Christmas gift for a member of the family that they could afford from the meagre contents of their piggy banks. A box of bath salts did for granny and mum was bound to appreciate a sweet smelling tin of talc. On Christmas Day he was thanked for his generosity and the 'smellies' were put into the bathroom cabinet alongside the identical ones he had got them for their birthdays.

The January sales were a special occasion when real bargains could be located, or so we thought. They were also an opportunity for stores to generate some business in the lull after Christmas when families usually tightened their belts having spent up buying presents for their children. We still have such sales, but their significance has been eroded by the frequency with which they seem to appear, especially when it comes to the likes of the big furniture chains that always seem to have offers that must end on Sunday. Which Sunday is less clear. Oldham Street's C & A, now sadly a defunct company, prided itself on offering a mixture of fashion and value and the crowds obviously agreed with that in 1948. Clothing was still rationed, as

can be seen from the poster offering certain items at half coupon rate, so items had to be chosen carefully. The number of shoppers wishing to take advantage of the sale had grown to such a crowd that the police were out in force trying to maintain some semblance of order, but they found a queue at a soccer turnstile easier to control than a mob of fashion conscious women. During the war they had suffered the constraints of utility clothing and short hemlines as material was preserved, but now they were ready for the romantic New Look designed by Christian Dior. Harold Wilson at the Board of Trade condemned it as frivolous, but women ignored him. What did he know about soft shoulders, handspan waists and full billowing, calf length skirts?

Above: From Pall Mall to Cross Street and the Royal Exchange beyond this section of Market Street was alive with shoppers in 1957. A solitary bobby walked up from the direction of Dolcis, passing the tobacconist who would blend a selection of aromatic pipe tobaccos just to a customer's liking. There were glass topped trays of the finest Virginian, Turkish and Balkan Sobranie varieties as well as speciality brands that included Three Nuns' round swirls of smoking pleasure. The shopkeeper even stocked thick twist for the hardbitten old timer who liked to cut a plug with his penknife before ramming it into the bowl of his pipe with a horned and blackened thumb. The clouds of smoke that engulfed a pipe smoker brought back memories of the Manchester

smogs, but the smell was surprisingly pleasant. You could always tell that a man smoked a pipe by the little holes in the front of his shirt where careless sparks had escaped from his briar. As the policeman continued on his beat people smiled and nodded a good morning. On the odd occasion we see a member of the law walking the streets now he is usually with a colleague for safety and if a pedestrian smiles at another person on the pavement he is thought to be odd or indulging in some form of harassment.

Top: In 1961 Marks and Spencer moved across the road to open this new store, seen here some two years after it opened. The bus is heading from St Mary's Gate and onto Market Street. Cross Street and Corporation Street run to the right and left on the other side of the department store. This building was one of many obliterated in the IRA attack on 15 June 1996 when a 3,000 lb car bomb exploded. A pillar box that somehow remained largely undamaged has since been resited on its original spot on the pavement on Corporation Street near to a memorial plaque. A new Marks and Spencer, the world's largest branch of this famous chain store with 32,500 square feet of floor space, has since appeared on the site and is connected to the Arndale Centre by a new bridge. However, half of the building has now been sold to Selfridge's. The man walking towards the camera is crossing Exchange Street which opens out into St Ann's Square. Behind him the woman keenly examining the jewellery in the shop window was possibly checking on the price and style of engagement rings as she might have been returning the following week with her intended. If she had left it 40 years until her return it would not have mattered. Kay's is still there, though the cost might have increased in the meantime.

Conran Street, at the corner with Carisbrook Street, close to its market, is in the heart of Harpurhey. Although added to the borough of Manchester in 1885 at the same time as Bradford and Rusholme, it has enjoyed keeping some of its own identity. Along with neighbouring Collyhurst, Harpurhey has regarded itself as being one of the places from where true Mancunians originate. Even as far away as Langley in Middleton the residents there still regard Manchester as their spiritual home, particularly if their families came from these streets at one time. Some of the famous names in soccer came from north Manchester, men who showed a determi-nation and true grit forged in more humble surroundings. It is no coincidence that Nobby Stiles, Paul Scholes, Tommy Booth and Brian Kidd sweated blood for City or United and none of whom could ever be called a shrinking violet. In 1959 we had come to the end of the grey days of shortages and tightened belts as goods were well within the price range that we could afford. Even items that were once luxuries, such as washing machines and televisions, were becoming standard equipment. We were still basically an honest set of people. Who today would leave a moped unattended outside a shop without padlocking it firmly to a drainpipe?

On the move

Traffic jams, crowded carriageways and vehicles grinding to a halt are not a modern phenomenon as can be seen from this 1939 scene. Market Street is now pedestrianised but it was once one of the busiest routes around the city. Great names along here at the time included Boydell Brothers' merchant tailors, the Albion Hotel and Yates Wine Lodge, but the women on the pavement were not interested in the last two of those establishments for they had shopping to do on what must have been a chilly day as they were well wrapped up against the weather. This used to be called Market Stead Lane and was part of the 18th century development of the town that spread eastward here and south along Deansgate. Many of the cars in the photograph had running boards, reminiscent of those used in gangster movies about the era when Al Capone or Legs Diamond sprayed their enemies with machinegun fire or when escaping from Eliot Ness and his Untouchables. The stern, rectangular lines of these old models are far removed from the sleek, swept back designs that we have now. Older readers may recall having to crank them into life with a starting handle in cold weather. Mum or one of the children pumped the accelerator pedal as dad turned the engine over in an effort to catch the very moment that it spluttered into life so that he could leap back into the driving seat before it died on him.

Above: E Simpson might have been a fine butcher but his grammar was not too good, as evidenced by the placing of the apostrophe in the lettering on the back of the van involved in this accident in 1943. That particular punctuation mark seems to have given people great problems for many a year. Just think of the number of little cafés that advertise 'tea's' or shops that are having 'sale's'. Yet adults today criticise the spelling and grammar of the young when their own parents were just as bad. But the Simpson van had more to worry about than dotting an 'i' or crossing a 't' because its bangers had gone off long before they

assistance and keep other traffic moving, though there were limited numbers of vehicles on the move because or rationing restrictions on fuel. From the angle of the vehicles it would seem that the lorry driver was at fault, having turned across in front of the van. Accidents at night during the blackout were quite frequent, but there was no such excuse in this case.

Top: The French have a saying that, in effect, means that even as life moves on in essence nothing really changes. That holds true for the city's transport system. In 1930 this tram stop on Oxford Road would have been viewed as a period piece half a century later, but in the 21st century it merely appears to be part of the evolution that has brought us the modern vehicles that criss cross the centre on a daily basis. The shape and lines of the coachwork may have altered but the basic job that they do in the field of public transport is just as it was. Unwary visitors to Manchester may be surprised to see tracks cutting across the roadway once again but Mancunians have become well used to their reappearance as part of the fabric of city life. Nostalgia buffs revelled in seeing the system reintroduced even if most of them were far too young to remember the originals that clanked their way backwards and forwards in a manner immortalised in song by the late Judy Garland's 'Trolley Song' in the 1944 movie 'Meet me in St Louis'. Perhaps some local film maker could produce a sequel, such as 'Meet me in St Peter's Square', though the title lacks a certain je ne sais quoi, to go back to French sayings once more.

reached the frying pan. The accident on Rochdale Road had occurred at the junction with Queen's Road, a notoriously dangerous crossroads in Collyhurst, just a couple of miles north of the city centre on the A664 heading out past Boggart Hole Clough towards Blackley. The police had turned out in force to lend

Above: The age of steam locomotives is one that fills most of us old enough to remember the puffing giants with a nostalgia that is fuelled by frequent trips down memory lane organised by railway buffs who have lovingly preserved old lines and rolling stock. Whenever there is an opportunity to see these marvels of engineering crowds gather to turn back the clock and gaze at the footplates wishing that they could step up into the cab and help stoke the boiler or pull on the whistle. Usually they have to be satisfied with short journey in one of the old carriages with the drop down sash windows. Sometimes Thomas the Tank and the Fat Controller are due to make an appearance and it is amazing how caring parents suddenly become. They decide that it would be a good day out for their children to visit Ramsbottom or Embsay and see these old locomotives in action. We know which ones are really the big kids. After all, was it not dad who bought that Hornby set for his two month old son last Christmas? He was trying to relive the day in 1957 when he got on board the excursion train at Victoria, piloted by engine 45642 'Boscawen'. The Victoria line was started by Manchester and Leeds Railway in 1844 and the station enlarged by Lancashire and Yorkshire Railway.

We cannot see what is in this young lad's left hand, but it could have been an exercise book in which he carefully recorded the engine numbers of the locomotives that thundered into Central Station in 1955. Now in his 50s does he still have that dog-eared record of the days he spent on such innocent pursuits tucked away in a tin box in the attic? Is it gathering dust along with other books full of cricket scores when he played imaginary matches for Lancashire as Geoff Edrich or Brian Statham using two small hexagonal metal rollers in a game called 'Howzat'? Up in the rafters there are Dinky cars, lead soldiers and a cap gun that are part of the culture of his childhood. Today, whenever he walks along Windmill Street he must feel a tingle looking up at the Great Northern Railway name that is still spelled out on the warehouse next to G-Mex, as the station became. Central Station was a magnificent piece of architecture that was completed in 1880 and included an impressive 210 foot roof span. There was a covered walkway across the street linking it directly into the Midland Hotel. Closure came in May 1969, by which time this boy's interests had moved onto more adult themes. After some time as a car park it became the exhibition centre and concert hall we have today.

But for the style of vehicle on Portland Street this could be a modern picture of traffic grinding to a halt instead of being set in 1955. The long line of buses shows how we still relied heavily on public transport to get us about because wholesale car ownership was not yet the norm, though the time when it became a necessity rather than a luxury was not too far away. The chap on the bicycle seems to have the right idea because at least he is on the move. This time of day is known as the rush hour, but it is not a description that fits easily with the scene of lines of gridlocked traffic. It would be more appropriate to call it snail hour as stationary exhausts pump out their toxic fumes into the surrounding environment. In the early 1950s these emissions, mixed with the smoke from factory chimneys and domestic coal fires, produced such filthy smogs that brought people with respiratory problems to their knees. A crisply starched shirt that was virgin white in the morning was a grey, black flecked caricature of its former self come night-time. Some of the buses on view had the letter X placed after their route number. This signified that they only operated during peak times and then just on the busiest part of the route.

Left: Rochdale Road in 1959 was unusually quiet. Even back then the scene was often busier than we can see here, though the amount of traffic today far outnumbers what we had in those 'never had it so good' times that Harold Macmillan liked to remind us of as he retained power in October's general election. He did have a point because we were becoming a more affluent society, as illustrated by the rise in private car ownership. With that symbol of good living came the problem of safety on our roads. Despite our scorn of the driving standards of Italians and the French, our own record was none too rosy. Back in the 1930s we had one of the worst set of casualty statistics in the western world, leading us to adopt various measures such as driving tests, pedestrian crossings and cats' eye road studs in an effort to improve matters. In the second half of the last century there were further road safety campaigns, such as the one in evidence here where motorists were reminded by placards to take greater care. In schools cycling proficiency schemes were launched and lessons given to children about the dangers on our roads via Stop, Look and Listen, the Tufty Club and the Green Cross Code. As television became a popular medium adverts were run, often using sporting personalities to reinforce the safety message.

Below: Parking was not too much of a problem near our football grounds in 1960, provided you set off early. At United's ground there was room on the railway lines alongside Trafford Park Road and near Maine Road there were innumerable little side streets where a lad would gladly keep an eye your motor for a few coppers. Not that he really did, but it was a way of ensuring that he had not scratched a rude message on the paintwork whilst you were preoccupied with watching Dave Ewing flatten yet another unwary centre forward. For those of us without cars or had left it to the last minute as we finished off a pre match pint and pie, there were the football specials. These buses on Aytoun Street were soon packed to the gunwales with supporters wearing coloured scarves, rosettes and waving rattles. When the final whistle blew it was a mad scramble back to where the transport was lined up, a quick push and shove and you were ready to be whisked back to the departure point and home in time to listen to what was left of Eamonn Andrews' 'Sports Report' before you read the Football Pink. Of course, all this took place on a Saturday, with the action starting at 3 pm. You knew where your team was in the league by teatime, rather than as happens nowadays thanks to the great god Sky that arranges games to suit its satellite fancy. You cannot imagine Harry Gregg saving a shot from Bill McAdams at 2.15 on a pay per view Sunday afternoon.

Right: The last of the trolley buses left Ashton under Lyne in 1966. We might have been winning the World Cup, but we were losing a form of transport that future generations will probably regard as a quirky piece of 20th century transport history. It was fitting that Ashton under Lyne corporation should send out this vehicle on its final journey as the first services were run along Ashton Old Road. With their arms reaching up to the power lines above they provided a natural link between the old tram system and the era of the petrol engined buses. After World War I it was appreciated that trams were too inflexible in dealing with the rising number of passengers and, as they were restricted by the tracks they followed, added to congestion on the streets as the motor car became more popular. It made sense to use some of the established cabling to power the trolley buses that could move more freely than their predecessors in public transport. For 40 years they were a common sight, though initially taking some getting used to. Pedestrians were accustomed to hearing the clanking of the trams as they approached and the quiet arrival of a trolley bus caught some unawares. Following a spate of accidents some dubbed them 'the silent death'. During World War II they became invaluable as many petrol buses were mothballed, their fuel being needed for the war effort.

Making a living

Above: A woman's place is by the kitchen sink, doing the housework and bringing up the children. Try and tell that to Louise Lyans as she received instruction from Jim Botterill in the art of driving a tram. She was Manchester's first woman tram driver, but was not really a trail blazer. Elsewhere women were driving ambulances, buses and jeeps in both military and civilian roles. The trend had begun in the 1914-18 War when women rolled up their sleeves and took over traditional positions on the factory floor and behind the wheel. Government had not given them the vote, but they rallied behind the flag in the service of the nation. It was even more apparent in World War II as munitions works, transport and agriculture all owed women a huge vote of thanks. The tram Louise was driving was the latest development from the one horse bus service from Pendleton to Market Street that first ran in 1824. Horse drawn trams operated from 1877 until 1903, being superseded by electric trams that continued to serve the city for nearly 50 years. When the first phase of the new supertrams was finished in 1991, linking Bury and Altrincham via Manchester, Louise might have been forgiven for regarding them as old hat. She had seen it all before from inside the cab.

It is remarkable that we managed to survive and even enjoy our lives before we had political correctness, equal opportunities and dictates against every -ism under the sun. Added to these is the health and safety lobby, possibly one of the nation's biggest growth industries of the last 20 years. The mind boggles at what it would have made of these workers at Manchester Abattoir in 1950. There is blood from the carcasses dripping all over the floor and stains on the men's so-called white coats. The flat hat never left the head of one member of this trio and rumour had it that he kept it on in the bath.

Imagine his attitude if he had to don a hairnet and put on a pretty white hat when he came to work. How times have changed, because even the humble butcher's shop no longer has rabbits and poultry hanging on hooks as they acquire an appropriately gamey smell. You cannot have a piece of corned beef stored within half a mile of a nice juicy sirloin and hands need washing so often that they end up looking as though they belong to Mrs Mopp. What was so wrong with wiping them on your overalls or picking up a chop dropped on the floor and giving it a quick rinse under the tap? A bit of sawdust put hairs on your chest.

Right: Even when middle aged a street trader was still referred to as a barrow boy. It was a hard life trying to make ends meet by attempting to attract custom to his humble point of sale in Market Place. He used a mixture of wit and vocal power to tempt shoppers his way, but, for the moment, seems to be taking a little rest in this 1958 photograph. That he dressed in a suit was not unusual because most men went into the city in those days much more formally dressed than ever they do now. It was not quite a pinstripe, but it was a jacket and trousers and he would have been horrified to come across a bank manager wearing what establishments refer to as business casual. To him it would have meant just plain scruffy. His body language suggests that his mind was elsewhere, perhaps offering up a silent prayer for the families of those players and officials lost in the Munich air disaster. He could also have been reflecting on the news that a new Pope, John XXIII, had been elected that year or wondering about the effect that parking meters appearing on London streets would eventually have on his home city. Behind him the new building work was only a foretaste of the changes to come on Market Place, that part of medieval Manchester that had been the scene of rioting against high bread prices in 1795. The cavalry quelled that disturbance, just as it did more dreadfully in the 1819 Peterloo massacre.

Below: After the first world war the government promised servicemen returning from their duties overseas that they would be coming back to a land fit for heroes. They were empty promises as the country nosedived into the years of economic depression that brought us a slump, strikes and hardship. Similar promises were made in 1945 and this time there was some truth in the assurances that were given, though it was hardly Utopia in the early postwar period. The electorate turned to Clement Attlee's Labour party to pave the way and the National Health Service came into being and immediate work began on restoring the nation's housing stocks. The prewar slums had become even worse in the intervening years and so many houses had been demolished in air raids that replacements were a matter of some urgency. At least Manchester could hold its head up high as it was one of the most farsighted of boroughs in the inter war years, building over 27,000 new council houses. Helped in part by American financial aid under the Marshall Plan, new homes rose from the ashes. Wythenshawe, part of the borough since 1931, was intended to be a largely self sufficient garden city, though it never quite achieved that aim in full. Here, in 1950, work was in progress building shops and maisonettes on Greenbrow Road, Newall Green. Many former urban dwellers got to enjoy front and back gardens for the first time.

Above: Hour upon hour of joy could be gained from browsing through the books piled high in Sherratt and Hughes on Cross Street. It was a comfortable place in which to spend an afternoon immersed in the language of the classic writers and those breaking into the world of popular literature. Georgette Heyer happily rubbed shoulders with Charles Dickens and there was an endless supply of Enid Blyton fare for the younger reader. Some visitors never bought a book but popped in from the office each lunchtime, read a chapter of a novel and returned on subsequent days until they had finished the whole book. Colonel John Hunt's 'Our Everest Adventure' was one of the bestsellers in 1954, recounting the conquering of the world's highest peak by the expedition he had led to the Himalayas the previous year. Sherratt and Hughes was also the bookshop where GCE 'O' and 'A' level students could buy their Latin primers, geometry books and log tables. It had a homely feel that only individual and independent shops can offer, but the days of the big chains did not just sound the death knell for family department stores and grocers. The arrival of companies like Waterstone's squeezed the trade for smaller bookshops and another familiar name on our shopping list was crossed out.

Below: There was a time when most women were able to make their own clothes, run up a set of curtains and make a set of cushion covers. In 1959 this pair was on Barlow Moor Road, Chorlton-cum-Hardy demonstrating the latest in the line of Singer models that was on the market. The woman on the left wore her dress at the fashionable mid calf length with a wide sweeping skirt over a petticoat that swung attractively whenever she did a twirl. By the end of the following decade skirts would be more like pelmets and the length of time it took to make a mini or micro shortened in direct proportion. Back home girls were taught to use knitting needles and interpret patterns and instructions such as 'psso' as they passed each slip stitch over. Socks were darned and elbow patches attached to dad's best jacket. If the slightest tear appeared in a piece of material it was out with the needle and thread or a quick treadle on the sewing machine to put it right. We now live in a throwaway society that has adopted the attitude of when it is worn then discard it. Our parents thought differently for they lived a life of make and mend. Mum could carry on a conversation, watch 'Emergency Ward 10' on the television and knit a pair of bootees for next door's new arrival all at the same time.

At first sight this appears to belong to a section on the wartime blitz, but the date is wrong as we are now in 1957. This fire at Paulden's department store on Stretford Road, next to Cavendish Street, destroyed a building that had stood on this spot since 1879. What a dramatic end it came to and what can better illustrate the courage of the firefighting crew than the sight of them striving to quell the flames as tons of masonry come crashing down around their ears. Their headquarters were on London Road, opposite the railway station, in that attractive baroque style building that was designed and built by Woodhouse, Willoughby and Langham from 1904-1906. Its

architectural merit was recognised by being given Grade II listed status. The central courtyard includes a training tower and a series of balconies in whose tenements 40 firemen once lived. The first fire brigades were run by insurance companies, anxious to keep a check on the high incidence of fire in our crowded towns in the early 19th century. The close proximity of properties to each other and the lack of common sense in taking safety precautions forced the insurers' hands as they were paying out with too much frequency for their liking. Eventually, local councils gradually assumed control and Manchester's own fire station was established in Town Yard where the town hall now stands.

The World's Market

suppliers of household products in the country. Now managed by George's middle son Ramesh the company is moving ever onwards with eldest son Sunder and youngest son Mohan based in the far east, a wide variety of products can be sourced for customers.

Trading as an importer, exporter, stockist and distributor the KB Group of Companies has a range of over 800 different items which encompasses household lighting, cookware, Christmas decorations, electrical goods, DIY and compact discs. By the close of the 20th century the small Manchester market stall had grown into a world wide business with an annual turnover of more than $200 million.

Though now taking a back seat George still regularly visits KB's North Street offices and keeps a relaxed overview of the direction the company is moving in today. No-one can ever say that turning a small business into a large one is easy, but TK 'George Khemlani' has dramatically proven that, though it may not be easy, with hard work it is certainly not impossible.

Left: *TK 'George Khemlani', company founder.*
Below: *Brochures promoting just a few of the company's products.*

Don't we all love to hear of the kind of happy story in which a local market trader makes good and expands his business from a simple market stall with just two employees into a globe spanning enterprise with hundreds of employees ? Of course that kind of growth does not happen without a vast amount of hard work and dedication.

In 1954 TK 'George' Khemlani was newly arrived from India and he was not afraid of hard work, or short of dedication to his small business, a market stall in Manchester. At the beginning of the 21st century his firm, by now the KB Group of Companies, would employ 3,000 people and have offices in Hong Kong, China - and of course Manchester.

Helped and supported by his wife Shoba and their three sons George developed his business into firstly a mix of retail and wholesale and eventually complete wholesale to become KB Import & Export Ltd. Established as a limited company in 1980 the company has since grown into one of the premier

Patterns of progress

From its small beginnings, more than half a century ago, JJ Harvey (Manchester) Ltd has gone from strength to strength in the development of precision tooling for the aerospace and automotive industry. Today the company boasts one of the largest purpose built tool-shops in Europe at its factory in Oldham Street, Denton.

The business had its origins at Christmas 1945 when Joe Harvey and a friend named Longstaff set up in business for themselves.

Joe had just finished training to be a Bevan Boy in a coal mine in Consett Co Durham. Bram Longstaff had been drafted in from Barrow in Furness for duty working in aircraft produc-

Below: JJ Harvey's staff pictured in 1955.

tion. This was at the time when the 'essential works' order allowed the Ministry of Labour to move people around wherever they were most needed.

The reason Longstaff and Harvey had started on their own was that another friend who worked in a local bakery was having big problems with spare parts. The oven door had become unusable and they were having problems replacing it. Longstaff and Harvey produced a wooden pattern and took it to a local foundry on a Saturday morning when they were open, got the casting done and then fitted the new oven door. Having completed this successfully they then had the idea of starting on their own.

Finding suitable accommodation was difficult. Joe and his wife, Constance, who had only married in the spring of 1945

had been fortunate in getting the tenancy of a two up two down terraced house. It was into the back bedroom of that house on Manchester Road, Heaton Norris, Stockport that they pulled up a bench through the window to start the business. Everything was to be done by hand as they had no machinery of any sort.

Obtaining orders was very difficult; war work had reduced dramatically and civilian work had not yet started in earnest. It was a hard time. Longstaff was in lodgings and each week the pair had to make sure they could cover their costs.

Constance worked as a sewing machinist and split her wage down the middle each week. Due to complaints from neighbours that they were working too late and keeping them awake, Joe and Longstaff finally found a small corner shop in Love Lane, Heaton Norris which had been empty throughout the war and had no windows. It was also a foot deep in rubbish which had to be moved before they began business. In Love Lane their first machine was a lathe bought with a £30 loan from Longstaff's prospective father-in-law.

Neither partner, nor their parents, had any previous business experience and they made many mistakes - buying things without receipts for example, so much so that came the year end, when they had to provide accounts, they finished up paying tax even though neither had taken anything like a wage from the business.

Another problem in the early stages was that one couldn't buy timber without a licence and you couldn't get a licence unless it was for essential work! To make do they bought scrap furniture and knocked it apart for the first 12 months or so.

Transport was another problem. Old wood was at first carried, and later pushed on a bicycle: next came an old motorbike and sidecar which had to be rebuilt before it could be used.

They tried a small advert in the Evening News which was spotted by an ex-foreman of Longstaff who was now working in a foundry pattern shop in Manchester. The owner of the foundry came to see them and agreed that he would give them around £50 worth of work each month. If the pair did more they got paid more, and less if they worked less, more or less to suit the foundryman and their capacity.

Once again however the pair had neighbour problems since they now had some basic machines and worked all the hours available.

Top: Early days in the workshop. **Above left:** *Coping with the delicate situation of getting finished products out of the second floor workshop at the Old Mill, Holt Town.*

The owner of the foundry - Sykes & Harrison Ltd - suggested that the pair joined him in business and he would give them all his work. Harvey and Longstaff agreed, and on a visit to the foundryman's accountants the company was formed, the foundry company having 80 per cent of the shares and Joe Harvey and Longstaff having 10 per cent each with a theoretical split of profits as and when they arrived.

The foundryman found an old building that had been an air raid shelter during the war. It was also windowless and full of rubbish. But they took it and opened their new business on the first floor. Soon they were widening their business taking in more work from larger foundries and work from some distance away including companies like Metropolitan Vickers (then a large electrical company with a foundry in Trafford Park).

When they moved into The Old Mill in Holt Town, Beswick they had six staff.

Top left: A complex pump with Suction Branch. ***Above right:*** *The premises on Blind Lane, Ardwick.* ***Right:*** *Patterns and core boxes for horizontal gas engines for the National Gas and Oil Engine Company in Ashton under Lyne.* ***Below:*** *Epoxy lining an Ingot Mould Pattern.*

The foundryman however soon sold his shares, along with his foundries, to an electrical company Switchgear & Cowan Ltd of Trafford Park and emigrated to Australia. This meant that the ten per cent shares were almost without value.

Meanwhile Longstaff had accepted a job with the foundries in Bangor, North Wales and became the works manager.

The new company used a process from America which was a cause of disagreement. This was made worse due to the fact that at the take-over by Switchgear & Cowan, Longstaff and Harvey had both had service contracts which included a clause forbidding them to trade in the same type of business within a radius of 50 miles of Manchester.

In 1952 Joe Harvey however made a new start in Blind Lane, Ardwick in a railway arch with a new partner, Vic Alfieri, and a labourer. With a family of three and Christmas a week away, and a distinct shortage of cash, it was a very unhappy period.

The new business was called the Pressure Cast Pattern Plate Co but quickly changed its name to Harvey and Pressure Cast Ltd so that the name appeared in the telephone directory next to what was then the competition.

Being next to a scrap yard was of great assistance since the company was able to buy scrap machines at very low prices. Joe Harvey was soon travelling 50,000 miles a year and at the same time trying to

contribute in the late evenings after returning from his travels.

Soon they needed more space and they were able to rent a room - an old building, at Lime Bank Street, being used as an ex-government surplus store and which was an old pickle works, home to Ally Sloper sauce. Most of the electrical conduit had been eaten away by acetic acid from the vinegar and provided some hair raising experiences!

As the company grew it was able to acquire additional rooms in the old building - with the one requirement that they had to remove all the rubbish from the site if they were going to rent. They got adept at the rubbish shifting business.

Years later the building was included in the plans for development and clearance in that area of the town. The company now started looking for premises in the north east part of Manchester since most of the staff would not have any transport problems there. They were fortunate in finding a new building in Oldham Street, Denton which had been built as a paper store for a cardboard box company which was operating on the site.

Top left and above left: New technology using Polyester Fibreglass Resin and Paper Honeycomb, for a six piece pump pattern for the foundry of Mather & Platt Ltd. Top right: The finished casting assembly. Right: Machining an Air Meter Mould for Technical Laminating.

With a loan of £12,000 from the bank the company was able to acquire the new building plus the allotments next door on which was constructed a wooden office leaving space for a further bay alongside the one originally acquired.

As time went by the company erected another second-hand building and at a later stage constructed a lean-to against the next door building and covered over a yard. After many years they finally bought the cardboard box company and the road which went down the side of the box works as well as the one that went along the rear of their premises and erected a concrete framed three storey office block.

Though the company started as wooden pattern makers it eventually moved on to using plastics, a process which gradually accelerated over the years; this was combined with the numerical control technology.

Before moving into plastics however the company first went into metal patterns in cast iron. It then changed direction and went into larger and heavier compression moulding tools -

the Sinclair C5 being a typical size of steel they were having to handle.

From the compression moulding tools they gradually moved into tools for carbon fibre, mainly in the production of aircraft panels like wing flaps, aerlerons and the tail planes.
The company's hallmark would become the size of work it was able to undertake, when the majority of competitors could only handle smaller products.

Twice during this period of growth however the business was on the verge of bankruptcy - the second time, with the help of consultants, they realised that they were trying to make too many products. The answer was to hive off the fibreglass department, which was moved out to Hyde and taken over by the then senior sales director Harry Hargreaves.

The firm had originally made wood patterns and metal patterns, they had then gone into cast die blocks using dies and moulds in cast iron and cast steel and were also producing large covers in fibreglass for use by the heavy electrical industry. They had also developed the technical side of the air meter construction for Rolls-Royce and a number of other areas for which they had been trying to develop including pressure cast plates. as well as working with gun-metal and aluminium.

Top left: Preparation work on an aircraft fuselage model. Above: The prototype ERF cab. Top right: Cast iron low pressure dies, for a Russian Project, on the firm's first N/C Machine. Right: A 30ft long test air intake rig for Rolls-Royce.

The foundry too was moved out also and it was decided to try and develop the heavy end of compression mould manufacture as a speciality, proposed by the Sales Director Laurie Ferrand. One of the innovative things would be the tooling for the new ERF truck Cab, the first by some years in mould application and the first all plastic cab internationally.

The existing works were surrounded on three sides by Lancaster Carpets who received an offer for the land and works, this offer was subsequently extended to include Harvey's premises. This enabled the firm to build a purpose-built factory on a green field site on the opposite side of Oldham Street. Harvey's was fortunate when building its new premises to be able to allow for the size, height, crane power and various other materials that were available to allow the company to make the best use of the facility. The first job on Harvey's 40 foot floor-borer was to numerically control and inspect a mould that was 30 feet long and 12 feet wide for British Aerospace; even now the number of companies able to handle a job of that size remain relatively few.

Of the staff Pat Mannion and Peter Timberlake would have an outstanding impact. Pat was a former Craven apprentice, Peter had served his time at Metrovik in Trafford Park. Another long serving member of staff who gave outstanding service was May Rutter, she was Company Secretary for many years, a demanding job amidst constantly changing circumstances.

Although over the years there have been many employees passing through the company the majority of the workforce have been long service people who have stayed with the company for the biggest part of their working lives meeting each challenge as it arose. Major challenges have been faced - the whole of the latter half of the 20th century was a period of constantly changing technology, materials and legislation.

Today the main markets are still mainly in the UK particularly the Aero industry: British Aerospace, Short

*Top: The company's premises pictured in the 1970s. It comprised a wooden office structure and underwent nine alterations over the years. **Above left:** An apprentice prize presentation by a National Union official and Joe Harvey. **Above:** A 40ft Horizontal Borer with N/C Retrofit. **Right:** Early use of Delcam Computer System for use in 3-D machining.*

Bros Belfast; Westland on the Isle of Wight and Marshalls, Cambridge UK - despite a great deal of competition from Europe and the USA.

Over the years the company has strongly believed in being a member of trade associations. At one time it belonged to the National society of Master Pattern Makers, the Institute of Foundrymen, the Engineering and Employers Federation and the Gauge and Toolmakers Association and visited many other trade associations in the same business through the International Trade Association.

Through these associations similar companies in the USA were visited a number of times by Joe Harvey and the Sales Manager, Norman Trelford, as well as ones in the Far East, Japan, Malaysia, Taiwan, Germany, France and Italy. Though involvement in these associations was a time consuming business it was well worth doing for the benefit of seeing how the other man did it, not least training staff.

Training is and has been a problem in achieving the numbers and quality of staff that is required and the skills that need to be applied. Joe Harvey was particularly interested in training and as a result he was eventually awarded with the MBE for his contribution to training.

Today, the firm still trades as Harvey Manchester Ltd despite changes in ownership. In the last 20 years the main sales have been in the production of steel moulds for the Autoclave vacuum forming of carbon fibre panels. New machines have been added and it now has one of the few facilities in the UK for this type and size of work.

High tide by the Ship Canal

In 1833 an English candle maker, William Procter, and an Irish soap maker, James Gamble, both living in Cincinnati, Ohio in the USA married two sisters. Four years later they formed a partnership which was to become the giant Procter and Gamble company.

The company grew quickly and in the late 1920s it contemplated its first move outside North America. Europe was still getting over the ravages of the Great War and many businesses were going through hard times. Thomas Hedley Ltd, a soap making company based in Newcastle, was one such organisation - though it was still in sufficiently good shape to ensure that that Procter and Gamble had to pay a million pounds for the business whose existing brands included the famous Fairy soap, a brand introduced as early as 1898.

Procter and Gamble took over Thomas Hedley & Co, founded in 1837, in 1930, though the Hedley name would be retained for some decades still to come. Many American brands were quickly introduced onto the British market. The new parent company's dynamic approach soon saw the Newcastle factory at full stretch so much so that a new site was needed. Trafford Park in Manchester proved to be ideal.

Below: *Trafford Hall as it was in 1896.*

The Trafford Park estates had been the site of Sir Humphrey de Trafford's mansion, but he had so disliked seeing merchant ships sailing past his property along the Ship Canal, constructed in 1894, that he sold the 1,200 acre estate - though not before building a ten foot high wall five miles long in attempt to hide the canal from his view.

Trafford Park was sold to a private company for £360,000. Eventually the park was sold by lots to any company that wanted to buy. Slowly the land nearest to the centre of Manchester became an industrial complex, though the western part of the Park would be undeveloped for many years: it was the site of the Royal Agricultural Show, a golf club, a horse market, stock yards, a polo ground and even , in 1910, an aerodrome. In 1931 ten acres were leased to Procter and Gamble at 9d a square yard. In 1933 that land was purchased outright.

The original factory took three years to build; at the time of its opening in 1934 it was the world's largest soap and candle factory.

The original products of household soap, candles and scouring powder grew and expanded to reflect consumers' increasing and changing demands. New brands were added, new buildings put up and additional land acquired.

By July 1940 Trafford Hall itself had been converted for use as a prisoner of war camp; during the night of 22nd-23rd it was badly damaged by a land mine. Another bomb came through the next door factory roof and landed in a frame of soap two floors below without exploding. Four men - Frank Poole (the works manager) Tom Alexander (who had just been blown 30 feet through the air when the land mine had exploded) George Harris and Tom Evans - coolly pushed the soap frame into the lift and took it out to the canal bank, so saving the factory from heavy damage. The fearless four were later presented with gold mementoes by the Managing Director at a ceremony held in the canteen. During the following night there was another potentially highly dangerous incident: a number of incendiary bombs fell on the roof of the factory's gas holder and another employee, Henry Galgut, climbed up and kicked them off one by one. On the morning of the 24th the main entrance to Trafford park was barricaded off because of the unexploded land mines and bombs lying around.

With its many factories Trafford park would be a prime target for the German bombers. When the air raid warning sounded most Hedley employees had to go into the air raid shelter under what would become the STU silo

unloading area. Only a few key operators would be left in the plant to keep the processes ticking over until the all clear sounded. Meanwhile air raid wardens would keep watch on the factory roof, one danger being that if one went to investigate a parachute seen descending in the night there might be a land mine attached to it and not a downed airman. When Henry Hickson arrived at the factory each morning his job was to go a round looking for unexploded bombs and incendiaries. One large pieces of shrapnel from a bomb which had exploded had flown in through a window and embedded itself in the in-tray on Dick Hall-Craggs, the Chief Engineer's, desk!

By now labour shortages were making themselves felt and although 530 employees were at work staff had to be brought down from Newcastle; able-bodied men were also recruited from the Irish Republic and for the first time married women were employed to ensure the continued production of 63,000 tons annually of Mirro, Oxydol, Sylvan Flakes and Fairy soap.

Top: Building of the factory still underway at the time production began in 1933.
Above: The only surviving image of the Candle Department which operated between 1933 and 1939.

On 9th February 1942 the Government introduced soap rationing. All British manufacturers' packs were now standardised: the four-weekly ration was one 8oz bar of toilet soap or one 12oz packet of soap powder per person (though there were extra rations for children, miners and chimney sweeps). For the next eight and a half years the Government controlled the manufacture of all soap.

What is perhaps not widely appreciated now, nor indeed even at the time, is how much soap and its component element glycerine contributed to the war effort. In wartime supplies of glycerine were of vital importance in the manufacture of explosives for shells and grenades. Hedley's process of glycerine recovery was so efficient that other firms sent their lye to London and Manchester for Hedley's to extract the glycerine for the Government. Soap too was very important - it was necessary for the maintenance of hygiene in bomb-damaged areas and in the theatres of war all over the world; soap was also used for cooling cutting tools on the lathes which made bullets and shells - and in addition up to 20 tons at a time were used for greasing the slipways each time a ship for the Royal Navy or Merchant

marine was launched. The supply of soap and glycerine was so vital to the country's war effort that Hedley's even manufactured competitors' products at nil profit while their bomb-damaged factories were being rebuilt.

At the end of the war in 1945 a Factory Victory Dance was held in the Longford Hall, Stretford and after almost six years of hardship the Hedley employees could enjoy themselves again. And the work would now be a little easier: that year the first power-driven fork-lift trucks were introduced. Now the heavy loads in the warehouse could be put on pallets and moved by machine instead of muscle power.

Top: *a group of salesmen and some of the Directors pictured on the day of the official opening of the factory on 6th April 1934.* ***Above right:*** *The four packing lines on the North end of the first floor.*

Industrial brands now being produced at Manchester included Olivso Bar, Trafford Bar, Cream Suds, Snowhite Flakes, Super Curd Flakes and Scourox. There was however still a world-wide shortage of oils and fats, and the soap ration far from ending after the war was actually reduced in June 1946 (it would not be until January 1949 that it would be restored even to its 1945 level). The Hedley Chemical Division therefore invented 'Freedom' a detergent washing up powder soon popular with housewives who wanted to double their soap ration.

In the Autumn of 1947 Dreft was reintroduced for use in hard water areas. Extremely popular before the war Dreft production had ceased in 1940 as some raw materials needed for its manufacture were unobtainable. Because No 1 Tower (the original Oxydol tower) had a stainless steel lining it was now converted at a cost of £33,750 to make Dreft whilst Oxydol production was switched to the smaller No 2 Tower.

Another welcome, or perhaps not so welcome, return after the war was the factory buzzer. Many factory hooters could be heard once more sounding over Trafford park to mark the start of the day's work. Each firm had its own sound varying from the deep-sounding many-toned buzzer at Metro-Vickers to the shrill, tinny notes from small engineering works. The Hedley buzzer was unusual in that it was sounded twice, once at five to eight and again at eight. It often happened that employees sitting in a bus near Carborundum Ltd would hear the first buzzer sound and then the progress of their bus would be stopped by a trainload of wagons crossing the road. The more athletic employees would jump off the bus and race

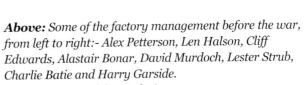

Above: *Some of the factory management before the war, from left to right:- Alex Petterson, Len Halson, Cliff Edwards, Alastair Bonar, David Murdoch, Lester Strub, Charlie Batie and Harry Garside.*
Below: *A view of the works in 1941.*

down to clock-in on time, whilst the less athletic sat in the bus knowing that they would be late.

In the late 1940s a major step was taken to modernise soap making. For nearly three years a new structure could be seen taking shape in the tankfield just east of the Kettle House. The main part of the equipment was a vertical tube 80 ft long. This structure was the latest method of producing soap - by hydrolysis. At very high temperatures and pressures oil and water reacted to produce fatty acid and sweetwater on a continuous basis. The fatty acid was then turned into soap. The new unit, the CSM (Continuous soap-Making Unit), started up in May 1950; at a cost of £200,000 it provided a great boost to productivity and also flexibility as soap brands could be quickly interchanged.

That same year a new Hedley product developed in Manchester named 'Tide' was produced in London. Tide caused a sensation, what one newspaper called 'the new washday miracle'.

Nor was Tide the only miracle of 1950: soap was de-rationed that September partly as a result of the pressure being taken up by new synthetic detergents. In anticipation everyone worked flat out to have stocks ready to meet the expected surge in demand with a long line of vans and lorries parked nose to tail along Trafford Park Road waiting to be loaded.

More expansion followed; the site of the old Trafford Hall was bought whilst more than half a million pounds was invested in a Tide production tower. The 1950s would see the introduction of many more new household names such as Flash and Fairy Snow.

By 1959 the company was producing eight times its initial output and employing 800

Top left: *The dry materials silo being welded into place near the Edible Bridge in 1968.*
Above right: *Emptying the 2-cwt bags of soda ash into the Mirro hoppers.*
Right: *Children enjoying the Punch and Judy show at one of the Factory's "Field Days" held between 1950 and 1974.*

people. New brands such as Fairy Liquid, Camay and Synthetic granules were introduced to meet the new demands of consumers. Other products such as Lenor and shampoo were moved to Manchester from other Procter and Gamble sites. Output from the factory would reach 166,000 in 1960. In 1962 another 23 acres of the park was leased, an event which coincided with an official name change from Hedley & Co Ltd to Procter & Gamble.

Over the next 30 years the Manchester site would change its product base many times. From soaps, edible oils - margarines and cooking oils -and washing powders to shampoos, conditioners and disposable nappies

reflecting the changing needs of customers and the company's willingness and ability to adapt to changing market conditions.

A new Paper Module opened in 1991 and 650 more staff were taken on. By the late 1990s the plant would have three modules: Paper, HABC (Health and Beauty Care) and Distribution. Now Procter and Gamble would expand once more with a major installation to manufacture Tissue Towel products.

By the end of the century the company would be employing some 700 staff and be producing more product per person than ever before.

Trafford Park with its road, rail and canal system significantly helps Procter and Gamble with its receipt of raw materials and the subsequent distribution of its finished products.

Procter and Gamble's continuing aim is to provide products of superior quality and value which improve the lives of the world's consumers. As a result consumers have rewarded the company with market leadership, sales and profit growth allowing its workers, its shareholders and the Manchester community amongst whom they live and work to prosper.

Today world-wide Procter and Gamble sells around 300 brands to some five billion consumers in more than 140 countries. The Trafford Park facility is one of more than 100 manufacturing sites operated by the company and now concentrates on family care products such as Pampers nappies, Bounty kitchen roll and Charmin bathroom tissue. The investment of £175 million in the early years of the new century, mainly to update tissue and nappy manufacture, has been matched by the highly capable and technically competent workforce - the key element which distinguishes Manchester from some Eastern European plants which operate with a low-skilled workforce. After massive investment over many years Procter and Gamble and its employees can be proud to have a fast moving, hi-tech facility with the capacity and capability to support its rapidly growing markets.

Above: A view of the site taken in the early 1980s.
Below: A recent aerial view of the site.

On the floor

Do you remember lino, how it cracked and broke and how we wished for something better. These days when we want a washable, flexible floor covering we choose PVC. In Britain the leading producer of PVC based flooring is the Polyflor company, the core business of the James Halstead group based in Whitefield.

Polyflor floor coverings have been around for a surprisingly long time, and the company traces its history back even further. Over the decades Polyflor has developed into a multi million pound specialist in vinyl floor covering materials and now occupies the leading position in its market. The company was the first to develop an unsupported homogenous vinyl floor covering suitable for commercial and institutional applications when it made the technical breakthrough in the early 1950s. In the following years the company achieved great

Top left: *Company founder James Halstead.*
Right: *A view of the spreading machines in the 1950s.*
Below: *The whole staff on their annual outing to Blackpool.*

market success and as a consequence of its strong position was subsequently able to establish overseas manufacturing facilities in Commonwealth countries such as Australasia and South Africa.

James Halstead Ltd was founded in 1915. The fledgling company was originally a weaving operation begun by the eponymous James Halstead. Born in Burnley in 1869 James had earlier worked for a relative's weaving firm in Bradford and later had a rubber department manager for J Mandelberg & Co Ltd in Manchester.

In 1915 James was already 46 years old and married to Grace Spencer; funding for his own business became available when his wife's brothers bought out her share of

and gents' waterproof clothing. In 1930 Belstaff would become a limited company taking its name from BELovitch and STAFFordshire where its roots lay. The Belstaff weatherproof suits rapidly became popular with motor-cyclists.

Back in Manchester James Halstead too had begun manufacturing motorcycle textiles in 1926. The original, material used was a double textured rubber cloth. Demand at the time was said to be 'most encouraging'.

James Halstead made its first flooring product in 1934. The company brought in a machine to friction calender (or roll) rubber onto a teased fabric. The material was very durable and did not need selvaging (edging to prevent fraying) and so was ideal for hard wearing applications. The material was sold to Briggs Motor Bodies (later bought by the Ford Motor Company) as carpeting.

the family business they owned. Now established in part of Crow Oak Works in Whitefield, near Bury, the product line was woven cotton textiles which were both dyed and waterproofed. Later the company was to turn to the production of rubberised fabric used in the manufacture of mackintoshes.

The first wages book showed just three staff, with the proprietor James Halstead drawing a mere ten shillings for his own expenses in the first nine weeks of business. By 1919 the company was enjoying a boom. With a rubber machine installed the company had expanded to three departments: proofing, weaving and rubber. More investment was made and the original share capital increased from £1,550 to £3,000 with James now owning 2,000 shares, Grace 900 and sons John and Herbert owning 75 and 25 shares respectively. By the end of 1919 more space was needed and the whole of the site was taken over.

Though staff numbers would increase they did so but slowly: James had a reputation as a patriarchal employer, each year he would send the staff on a day trip to Blackpool - all of them carried in a single charabanc.

Meanwhile in 1924 Eli Belovich formed a clothing company in which he would later be joined by his son-in-law Harry Grosberg. Based in Stoke-on-Trent the company made capes, leggings, rucksacks, haversacks and ladies

James Halstead, the company founder, died in 1935 at the comparatively young age of 66. He left the company in the hands of his two sons, John and Herbert. John, the elder son, was a gifted salesman. Herbert, the younger son, was a steady 'methods' man and not one to waste words - once in need of his brother who was then overseas he sent the memorable three word telegram 'John. Come. Herbert.'. With complementary skills, together they formed a good partnership.

When the second world war began in 1939 a massive demand was created for both Halstead and Belstaff products. The army needed

Top left: Machine No 4 producing cable compound for BICC for insulating cable.
Above: An early Polyflor delivery vehicle.
Right: Protective motorcycle clothing from 1956.

ground sheets, tarpaulins, rucksacks and the two companies were kept very busy on war work.

When peace returned in 1945 the two companies got back to peacetime manufacturing. But raw materials - especially rubber were scarce. The Halstead company now experimented with new materials, particularly PVC, to try and create a plastic floor. Eventually they succeeded with a unique formula which would give birth to Polyflor sheet vinyl flooring.

During the war the company's friction calender had lain idle but shortly after the war the company employed a chemist, Bill Roberts, who had been developing a new polymer called PVC at the giant Imperial Chemical Industries (ICI). Roberts began to experiment on the calender although the development was impeded by the fact that the machine had been designed for rubber rather than plastic. Roberts began by friction calendering a thin layer of marbleised PVC compound on to bitumen paper.

One of the difficulties he could not solve was the 'lay-flat' problem: in other words the flooring would wrinkle. The only solution was to

cut the sheets into tiles, but the company did not want to sell tiles which were then subject to tax.

Roberts persisted; he tried adding wood flour and cork to the formula but when this got wet it absorbed moisture and began to curl. Eventually Roberts tried calcium carbonate or limestone to the recipe and developed a formula that is very similar to that used to this day though every element except the limestone has since been improved in some way.

In 1948 Belstaff joined the James Halstead Group of companies which now became a public company. Floated on the Stock Exchange on 30th April 1948.

Top: Tempo coming off the line. **Above:** *The firm's original Crow Oak Works.* **Left:** *Geoffrey Halstead with Ken Entwhistle (Export Director) with a board of trade official in the 1960s.*

The first Black Prince motorcycle suit would appear in 1953. This was made at the Silverdale factory which had been set up a year earlier. The suit would become a classic design that was to stay in production for over 20 years with sales reaching a peak of 40,000 suits a year.

And now the group expanded its flooring business. In 1954 a major push behind that fledgling area resulted in fast growth. About this time the very first installation of Polyflor was carried out by Robert Kerr a leading Manchester flooring contractor . The group continued to invest heavily in flooring encouraged by a report from the Building Research Station which described the material as '...comfortable and quiet to the tread, not readily stained and not difficult to clean and maintain...'

Growth in this period led to the establishment of a holding company to separate the trading activities of James Halstead Ltd from the financial activities of the whole

group. In November 1962 James Halstead (Holdings) Ltd came into being.

The group would go on to open manufacturing ventures in South Africa, Australia and New Zealand in 1963. Such was the demand for the new products that the group created overseas manufacturing and sales operations that reached right around the globe. But by the end of the 1960s the international market had changed with stiff competition arising and the benefits of single site product development and manufacture would result in a refocusing on the UK operation.

Before that refocusing began however John Halstead died, having passed away in 1965. Initially he was succeeded by a team of professional advisers who were later replaced by Geoffrey Halstead.

These were the most difficult and worrying years the company would experience; the investments in South Africa had been catastrophic whilst the Australian company had fallen into loss. Management consultants were brought in who recommended amongst other things bringing in a Group Managing Director from outside the Halstead family.

Sadly matters only improved temporarily under new management. All overseas manufacture

Top right: Part of the textile warehouse and distribution area in the 1950s. Above left: The very first Conway Trailer Tent. Left: Mr and Mrs Geoffrey Halstead presenting the winners prize of a Polyflor sponsored horse race at Perth Races.

had ceased by 1971 and profits began to rise only for the national economy to be brought to a juddering halt and even thrown into reverse by the oil crisis of 1973 - especially Halstead's whose raw products were largely oil based. Major losses were incurred.

In the years following Herbert Halstead's death in 1974 (which led to the retaking of control by the family) Geoffrey Halstead went on to build a new team of highly professional and effective managers who would set the pace for continuing growth.

By 1980 the group's sales would exceed £21 million annually; by 1990 turnover was £57,985,000.

That growth included acquiring the Conway company of Wigan. Conway was a private company that had manufactured touring caravans and poultry cages. The growth in leisure in the 1960s and the firm's expertise with sheet metal fabrication, joinery and cabinet making made its move to manufacturing trailer tents in 1968 a natural extension. In 1980 the Halstead group took over Conway and within a couple of years the firm was offering luxury features such as fridges and top quality upholstery never before seen in the folding camper market. Four years later Conway would diversify into light industrial trailers. Prompted by of the seasonal nature of camping and consequent fluctuations in demand for its products, Conway began the manufacture of its Glidalong range of low loaders, tippers and platform trailers.

Meanwhile, with increasing car ownership and a fall in sales of motor cycles (and therefore protective clothing)

Belstaff diversified too. Belstaff began to produce leisure clothing introducing a range of golfwear, classic country wear and fashion outerwear for all kinds of leisure pursuits. The victorious Ryder Cup team of 1985 would be clothed in Belstaff golfwear. That diversification would, in 1989, see the James Halstead Group acquire Australia's Driza-Bone company, one of Australia's most famous names in weatherproof clothing. The Driza-Bone was originally designed at the end of the 19th century as a stockman's raincoat and was first made in Australia by Thomas Edwin Pearson; it would soon become a much sought after fashion accessory following Halstead's acquisition of the company together with manufacturing capacity at its Brisbane factory.

In the late 1980s the group was not however solely focused abroad. In 1986 James Halstead Ltd launched its Polysafe safety flooring. At the same time Conway introduced a new

Top right: An aerial view of the works in 1993. *Above:* Geoffrey Halstead and Michael Vale (Export Director) with Chinese visitors. *Left:* Geoffrey Halstead at a fund raising event for Manchester's Olympic 2000 bid.

commercial sector and is well understood by the marketplace, whereas many larger competitors have a confusing array of products representative of their multi site operations

The Halstead family remain major shareholders; at the start of the third millennium Geoffrey Halstead is company chairman with Mark Halstead, the fourth generation, in the business leading the firm as its Chief Executive.

The home market is served by a technical sales force of 25 whilst all production is carried out in Whitefield. Some 500 people are employed at Whitefield where the company has invested some £30 million over fifteen years in order to maintain the technical superiority of its products and remain competitive world wide.

anti-vandal portable accommodation unit; a new, high specification modular design and a rugged product which opened up a new market for Conway. The portable buildings could be used by local authorities, public utilities, construction companies and general industry. In the final year of the 1980s James Halstead would launch yet another new flooring range this time its Finesse and Panache ranges offering non directional floor covering.

The future of the James Halstead group was however firmly in floor coverings. Though textile production ended in 1992 throughout the 1990s sales rose from £58 million to £84 million, and would rise even further in the early years of the new millennium.

Concentration on floor covering products and the group's core business Polyflor Ltd, would lead to ending the operations of Belstaff, the sale of Driza-Bone in 1999 and finally the sale of Conway (by then renamed Titian CPL) in 2001.

Today half the company's output is exported all over the world for installation in hospitals, schools and public buildings much of which is sold through subsidiary companies in Australia, New Zealand, Hong Kong, Germany, Norway and Eire.

Polyflor is one of the smallest vinyl flooring manufacturers in world terms which still enjoys independence. All its competitors are multi-nationals, but the retention of its independence and its relative small size has enabled the company to react quickly to market situations and to retain flexibility. The company's broad yet comprehensive range of products is highly focused on the

The company would certainly have difficulty trying to fit all its employees into a single charabanc today!

Top left: The site pictured in the mid 1990s.
Right: Chief Executive Mark Halstead. Below: The company's board of Directors.

Cooee Mr Shifter

'Dad, do you know the piano's on my foot?' - 'You hum it son and I'll play it'. Now there's an advert that no-one will ever forget!

When it comes to making a pot of tea 'Brooke Bond' is one of the world's best known names. Yet Brooke Bond has its origins firmly rooted in Manchester; it was in 1869 that Arthur Brooke first opened a shop in the city selling his own blends of tea, coffee and sugar. There never was a Mr Bond: according to Arthur Brooke it sounded so well that he simply added it to his own name to complete the company's title.

Arthur Brooke was born in 1845 above the family shop in George Street, Ashton-under-Lyne; his father, Charles Brooke, was a tea wholesaler. Despite his father's trade young Arthur entered the cotton industry - though soon leaving that business when, at the age of 19, the mill in which he was a partner failed due to the disruption of supplies of raw cotton during the American Civil War. Arthur then went to Liverpool and later London working for Peek Bros. & Winch, a wholesale tea company, before eventually returning home to help his father.

Arthur Brooke began his own business at the age of only 24 using £400 saved from his share of the profits from his father's firm. His first shop was at 29 Market Street, Manchester. Above the shop he hung his now famous, if inaccurate, sign Brooke, Bond & Co.

Arthur revolutionised the trade, selling tea, coffee and sugar for cash only: that policy enabled him to keep his prices low and quality high as his business was not hampered by credit and debts.

Above: *Arthur Brooke, founder of the company.*
Below: *St Dunstan's saleroom.*

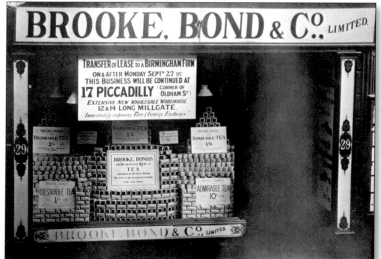

criminal offence to imitate a competitor's product forging his signature certainly was.

Arthur Brooke quickly gained a reputation amongst both the public and grocers, some of whom began to ask if they could buy his tea in bulk. More shops were soon opened in Liverpool, Leeds and Bradford. In 1872 Arthur moved to London establishing a warehouse in Whitechapel High Street which became the company offices.

Despite setbacks, including the failure of two shops in London and the poor management of the Liverpool shop run by Arthur's brother-in-law Arthur Bushell, nevertheless by the age of 30 Arthur Brooke was making £5,000 a year. Arthur had become a rich man. In 1875 he married a naval captain's daughter, Alice Catherine Young, and set up home in Stonebridge Park, Willesden.

Rather than sell loose tea from chests, Arthur Brooke developed his own quality blends by mixing various teas to give a more consistent taste. This became the principle which would later lead to PG Tips and other favourite blended brands. Tea was sold in 1/2lb and 1lb paper bags; in the shop window Arthur put a mechanical wooden figure known as Jack, which both advertised his wares and attracted passing custom.

In order to guard against competitors imitating his products each tea packet was printed with 'Brooke Bond & Co' in Arthur's flowing script. This not only made the product instantly identifiable but for over a century also served as a trademark - since although it was not a

In the late 1870s a trade depression hit Britain and the tea business ran into serious trouble; shops in Scotland had to be sold and Arthur had to sell his home and move to a smaller property in Bedford Park. The tide turned when Arthur recognised the potential of selling his tea in bulk, wholesale direct to grocers - though on a cash with order basis. Becoming both a retailer and wholesaler enabled the business to survive and by 1887

Top: *Early modes of delivery.*
Above left: *The shop at 29, Market Street*

Arthur was able to buy a house in Kensington and a country house near Dorking.

In 1892 Brooke Bond became a limited company with a share capital of £150,000. The business was by now largely wholesale with the advantage that unlike other firms the business did not need to employ travellers or 'reps' but instead relied on its fine reputation to obtain orders.

Competition demanded a cheaper blend of tea however. In 1898 Brooke Bond launched a 'True Tea' at 10d(4p) a pound. In 1899 Gerald Brooke, Arthur's eldest son, joined the business and found himself packing tea in Leeds. It was a baptism of fire. Despite the hard work however there was never a shortage of people willing to work for Brooke Bond: Arthur was a generous employer being one of the first to give his workers bonuses and to reduce the working day to eight hours.

Arthur was also generous to his customers; in 1899 for example, the year of Queen Victoria's 80th birthday, he gave all regular customers over the age of 80 one pound of tea free.

The company widened its horizons when at the turn of the new century it looked to add the Indian market to its overseas interests. In 1902 that ambition was realised with winning the contract to supply tea to the Delhi Durbar.

By 1905 Arthur Brooke was looking forward to retirement but misfortune struck: a serious misjudgment of the Calcutta market resulted in disastrously reduced profits. Arthur was forced to delay his retirement and to recruit additional help to strengthen the sales and purchasing side of the business.

This page: *HRH Prince Philip pictured during his visit to the factory in 1965.*

Gerald Brooke did eventually succeed his father as company chairman, but not until 1910. The first years of his chairmanship saw the start of mechanisation; Brooke Bond also began using motor vans in place of horse-drawn vehicles to distribute its goods.

Following the outbreak of the first world war in 1914 tea imports were curtailed by the government. Gerald Brooke instantly turned over to coffee and sales were healthy. Public outcry however soon led to a reversal of government policy and the restriction on tea imports was relaxed.

With the end of the Great War in 1918 tea sales continued to grow and outpaced existing production facilities in London and Manchester. A new purpose built tea-blending and packing factory was constructed in Trafford Park 1922. Sadly Arthur Brooke did not live to see the new

development: he died on 13th April 1918 leaving a considerable fortune.

In the 1930s tea was often sold for its claimed medicinal properties. One blend was promoted through a campaign aimed at doctors and nurses on the

strength of its properties as an aid to digestion. Some early adverts contained references to the qualities of 'digestive' or 'pre-gestive' tea.

Legal objections were soon made to these unsubstantiated medical claims and to the use of the word 'digestive'. John Peel, Brooke Bond's home sales director countered this challenge by inventing the name 'Pre-Gest-tea'. Bulk packets of Pre-Gest tea bore the letters 'PG' and the blend soon became known in the trade simply as 'PG Tips' since only the tips of the tea bush were plucked. This soon became the brand name which has survived to the present day.

In 1955 PG Tips became the feature of an amusing and unusual advertising campaign which was to become one of the most successful in the history of television.

It was Bill Barter of Spottiswood's advertising agency who suggested that chimpanzees be used in a television commercial. Chimps had a long association with tea due to the long-running 'Chimps Tea Party' at London Zoo which was hugely popular with both adults and children alike.

The first two television commercials produced for Brooke Bond were 'Stately Home' and 'Chimps Tea party' featuring the Marquis troupe of chimps trained for cabaret by Gene Detroy. That first ever Brooke Bond TV commercial was broadcast on Christmas Day 1956 and featured the chimps sipping delicately from bone china cups in an elegant country mansion.

A further series featured chimps from Billy Smart's Circus. The popularity of the commercials exceeded all expectations with voices provided by such famous names as Peter Sellers, Bruce Forsythe and Bob

Top right: Arthur Brooke's statue in the Trafford Centre.
Above left and left: Modern production facilities in the Brooke Bond factory.

Monkhouse. Very quickly the commercials became so popular that the chimps were soon in great demand for public appearances.

Probably the most famous and successful troupe of chimps used in the adverts were now discovered and signed up by Brooke Bond. These chimps were owned and trained by Molly Badham and, as well as appearing in television commercials, they made public appearances around the country opening supermarkets and new stores. They even attended a Brooke Bond staff party held to mark the retirement of Lillian Bristow as advertising manager; there Johnny, Judy, Sam and Rosie proved popular and charming guests, with Rosie demonstrating a particular liking for gin and orange along with almond icing!

The success of the PG Chimp commercials certainly helped Brooke Bond sell more tea. By 1957 the advertising budget had reached an incredible £680,000 but that high cost was more than offset by the increase in tea sales: the company could now say that one in every four families in Britain was drinking Brooke Bond tea.

As well as opening supermarkets the chimps also appeared live at Saturday morning film shows staged by the company's own projection units which, during weekdays and evenings, also presented documentaries to schools and institutions all over the country.

Probably the best remembered advert of the series is 'Mr Shifter' the saga of the removal firm and a piano stuck on the stairs. That advert has been on television more times than any other commercial earning itself a place in the Guinness Book of Records.

In the 1980s the series departed briefly from its 'slice of life' approach with the launch of the spy-thriller spoof starring 'Bond...Brooke Bond'. That all-action hero was briefed by the British Secret Tea Service to safeguard the secret of PG Tips. Those adverts saw 'Bond' skating over frozen lakes and leaping barriers as well as sauntering down the platform at 'Instant-bul' to board the Leyton Orient express.

Top right: *Modern packaging facilities.* ***Right:*** *Staff gathered together at the Reebok Stadium.*

The decade of the 1980s saw the celebration of 25 years of the PG Chimps TV commercials. That anniversary was celebrated in style in January 1982 with a party attended by Brooke Bond, Cyril the Cyclist, scriptwriter Tony Toller, voice-over stars such as Irene Handle, Pat Coombs, Keith Connor and John Junkin as well as an ITN film crew and over 40 reporters.

The 1990s saw the return of the 'slice of life' series with the saga of the Tipps family: Geoff, Shirley, Kevin and Samantha. In 1996 the PG Chimps celebrated 40 years in the advertising business. Commemorative merchandise included calendars, tea cards and cuddly toy chimps. Although the chimps ads still remain extremely popular it has been recognised that after 45 years there was a need to

introduce a specific ad campaign that will help modernise PG Tips and get people to re-appraise tea.

In January 2002 a series of adverts were screened introducing the T Birds. The adverts follow the ups and downs of tea drinking Maggie, Tom, Pete and Holly as their feathers are ruffled and soothed again with a "PG moment". Produced by Aardman, the Academy award winning creators of Wallace and Gromit, Chicken Run and Creature Comforts, the adverts are humorous and enduring, and appeal to all ages and especially the younger generation.

Today the Brooke Bond Tea Company is part of Unilever Bestfoods the largest food company in the UK with nine major sites across the country. The factory in Trafford Park employs around 400 people manufacturing and producing tea products including PG Tips, Brooke Bond D, Scottish Blend and Choicest Blend. The secret of the firm's continuing success still lies in the expert selecting and blending of teas so that each brand retains its own distinctive flavour and character. Brooke Bond selects tea from around the world, including its own plantations, so the company's expertise is based on a deep understanding of the tea plant itself: growing, preparation and blending - the whole process from bush to cup. A complete manufacturing operation is performed in Manchester from receiving the goods raw in chests and bags to packing them into finished articles ready for the shops.

Trafford Park is the most advanced tea manufacturing plant in Europe. Investment in new technology has been the key to maintaining that position in addition to keeping costs low and quality and customer service high. By the start of the new millennium extensive investment had taken place to upgrade facilities and install unique machinery to produce the Pyramid tea bags which would prove to be a huge success in national sales in the UK and in other countries in Europe.

At Trafford Park around 200 million tea bags and nearly half a million packets of loose tea are packed every week. Nationally we drink enough PG Tips every day to fill six Olympic-sized swimming pools! Proof positive that Manchester's Brooke Bond cuppa remains the most popular drink in the UK. The firm has certainly come a long way since Arthur Brooke opened his small shop in Market Street back in 1869!

Top: The current premises at Trafford Park Road.
Above: Maggie, Tom and Pete (back) and Holly (front) from the advertising campaign which began in January 2002.

Engines of progress

The name of Rolls-Royce resounds around the world as the very acme of engineering excellence. When, in 1989, that name was linked with that of the great Manchester engineering firm of Crossleys the result would be an inevitable triumph.

The famous Crossley family had owned two principal companies in Manchester. The first and most important was Crossley Brothers Ltd, manufacturers of gas engines, gas plant, stationary and marine diesel engines, which had been started in 1867.

The second company was Crossley Motors Ltd. Formed in 1910 it traded until 1958 and was dormant from then until 1968 when it was renamed Leyland National Ltd.

Two Irish brothers Frank and William Crossley moved to Manchester in their twenties and started their own

Above: An engraving of the Crossley works from the early 1900s. Right: The 4-stroke 'Otto' cycle. Below: The Crossley Scavenge Pump Diesel, a new type of marine engine being tried out in a Lowestoft trawler in July, 1933.

business in Great Marlborough Street making rubberised cloth for Mackintoshes. The two entrance streets to the works would eventually be named Frank Street and William Street.

The first company's product range quickly expanded to include small hydraulic presses and steam engines. In 1876 William married and travelled to Germany on honeymoon; there, by chance, he met Dr NA Otto who had developed the four stroke version of the compression-ignition gas engine. The 4-stroke 'Otto' cycle became the basis of the modern internal combustion engine and the astute Dr Otto had the world-wide rights.

Powered by coal gas the engine was much more efficient than the steam engine and William instantly saw the commercial possibilities. Forgetting his bride (though not entirely for their son Kenneth was born in February 1877) William sent for his brother and they quickly negotiated

In 1880 the Crossley brothers acquired a new site in Pottery Lane, Openshaw. Wealth now allowed the brothers to become prominent philanthropists, helping pay for such institutions as the Lads' Club at the Pottery Lane works, Star Hall in Pollard Street and the Crossley Nursing Home in Ancoats.

In the 1890s Crossleys began to produce both petrol and diesel engines as well as gas plant. A further factory was opened in Napier Street, Gorton Lane. The company's offices were in County Buildings, Cannon Street, though they also owned 8-10 Cross Street - which would be leased to Boots from 1925 until it was demolished to make way for the Arndale Centre.

The company's first motor cars were assembled at a factory in City Road, Hulme, though production later moved to Gorton.

Frank Crossley died in 1897, his brother William, however, lived on until 1911, having been MP for Altrincham from 1906 until 1910 when he was elevated to the House of Lords. On Sir William's death his son, Sir Kenneth Crossley, took over the companies.

exclusive rights for use of the engine throughout the world except for Germany.

By 1877 the brothers obtained rights to the German 4-stroke internal combustion gas engine which became a major product. Another memorable product, though one which is unlikely to be returned to, was Crossleys' patent Thistle Cutter, a device having no moving parts but with the capacity to cut up to 12 acres an hour of the dreaded thistles.

Crossley Brothers Ltd now concentrated on gas engines, mainly used to generate electricity, although by the 1950s it would also become heavily involved in building engines

Top left: Open Day visitors being explained the machining of large crankshafts. ***Top right:*** Children of employees at Openshaw enjoy a Christmas Party. ***Above left:*** One of the Crossley cars. ***Right:*** One of the 1,175 buses that Crossley's exported to Holland following the second world war.

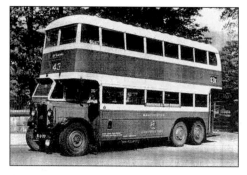

for railway locomotives. Crossley Motors Ltd became a separate company.

Meanwhile the other business, Crossley Motors, had its own parallel history, with its distinctive trademark, the Coptic Cross, an oblique reference to the Crossley name. Having made some large cars before the first world war the firm moved into manufacturing for the forces and thousands of staff cars were supplied in addition to the RFC Tender - a general purpose light lorry and ambulance, some fitted with half tracks, whilst more still were built in Russia under licence. De Havilland Aircraft, too, would be produced by the factory.

Following the war many of the ex-RFC vehicles were converted to charabancs and sold as small buses. Crossley cars, however, remained popular too and were turned out in large numbers even into the hard times of the 1930s: around 19,000 cars would be produced between 1904 and 1938.

Cars were not, however, particularly profitable, and it was in fact orders for buses from Manchester Corporation

which formed the core business. It was Manchester Corporation's orders which carried the firm though the 1930s, with 90 per cent of bus sales going to the city.

The bus venture required extra space and in 1928 new bodyshops were built in Crossley Street - the factory, known as the Crossley Street Works, was eventually demolished in 1990.

By the mid 1930s Crossley Motors had built more diesel buses than any other firm in the world, more than a thousand being eventually operated by the Manchester Corporation alone. Unfortunately Crossley buses would suffer serious mechanical failure every 50,000 miles or so compared to Leyland and Gardner engines which could run for 130,000 miles. Despite these problems the production of Crossley cars would cease in 1937 in order for the firm to concentrate exclusively on buses, and not just diesel buses.

Paradoxically other engines were arguably being built too well! The famous star ferries which ply Hong Kong harbour for 20 hours a day every day of the year are powered by 30 year old Crossley H-type two-stroke diesel engines produced in great quantities from the early 1920s until the 1960s. Similarly the Mersey Ferries would use Crossley engines more than 30 years old.

Top left: *A Crossley Condor Trolley Bus.*
Top right: *Manchester Corporation bus number 2128. This is a 1948 Crossley DD42/75 with a Crossley H32/26R body, pictured in Piccadilly, Manchester in 1965.*
Left: *A Rolls-Royce engined Star ferry at work in Hong Kong Harbour.*

Crossleys also built trolley buses too and received its first order from Manchester Corporation in 1937. Crossley Street works was extended in 1937 but the greatly increased volume of orders for military vehicles, in the run up to the second world war, soon caused bus output to drop behind schedule and the Corporation began to order from Leyland and Daimler.

All was not lost, however, and in 1944 the prototype of Crossleys many successful post-war bus bodies made its first appearance on Manchester's streets. And immediately after the war Crossleys celebrated the receipt of an order for no fewer than 1,175 buses to replace those destroyed in Holland.

In 1947 the company sold its works at Gorton and moved to its other works at Errwood Park at Heaton Chapel, works which had been occupied by the Ministry of War for several years.

Capacity at Errwood Park allowed for production of up to 400 buses a year, but with much reduced sales to Manchester Corporation the future no longer looked rosy. In 1948 the company was sold to AEC Ltd and the name changed to Associated Commercial Vehicles Ltd.

From the early 1960s Crossley would build, under licence, the world famous SEMT-Pielstick PC range of engines. Producing up to 10Mw each and weighing 100 tonnes the PC2 engine would be not only the firm's largest but also its best selling engine. More than 240 of these engines would be put into ships and power stations around the world with sales to the Royal Navy and Sealink. The world's navies were also keen to buy the smaller, lighter SEMT-Pielstick PA6 range of engines.

The latest addition to the Rolls-Royce range of diesel engines is the Allen 5000 series which is the most powerful medium speed engine of it's size available. Designed predominantly for the power generation market with a power output of 500KWe per cylinder, low fuel consumption and low emissions, showing Roll-Royce commitment to the environment, this engine will keep the Crossley name going into yet another century.

The Crossley name has now all but disappeared, replaced by the even more prestigious name of Rolls-Royce. In 1968 the company was acquired by Amalgamated Power Engineering (APE) and the name became APE-Crossley Ltd. APE in its turn became part of Northern Engineering Industries (NEI) who were in 1989 subsequently taken over by Rolls-Royce and the company is now a division of Rolls-Royce Power Engineering Plc. Part of the original factory however is still in use as the UK centre for the parts and aftersales market and still retains the name of 'Crossley Works', testament to the determination and vision of the two brothers, Frank and William who left Ireland, to make their fortune, in the 1860s.

*Top left: HMS Ocean, powered by Rolls-Royce engines manufactured at the Crossley Works. **Top right:** The latest engine to be manufactured at the Crossley Works, the Allen 5000 series. **Left:** One of Crossley's SEMT-Pielstick PC engines.*

The man who built a building empire

Few of today's generation of aspirational captains of industry - certainly not the high-tech whiz-kids - will get their hands dirty building up their companies, as Roland Bardsley literally did to create his construction conglomerate.

And fewer still of the post-Millennium business 'brats' will have any inkling of the sheer physical blood, sweat, toil and tears demanded in establishing the foundations of one of Britain's most respected homes building-to-commercial contracting and leisure empires.

Today the trademark blue-and-white Roland Bardsley logo is a familiar motif on busy constructions sites throughout the North of England. However, it is not a mere corporate symbol, but a guarantee of style, elegance, quality and finesse - those traditional virtues Roland prized highest in his quest to provide outstanding value for money in everything his companies undertook in the forty odd years he held the reigns.

His building work was consistently recognised by a tide of glittering awards, not least of which was that from the Government-sponsored National Housing Forum, in 2002, whose survey of 10,000 home-buyers voted Roland Bardsley Homes one of Britain's top house-builders and Best in the North West.

So, unsurprisingly, a Roland Bardsley-built home is worth every penny of the premium it often fetches, so thoroughgoing is its quality of workmanship, so consummate is the craftsman's attention to the fine detail within.

Above: *Company founder, Roland Bardsley.*

But little is known of the business buccaneer and building pioneer whose genius at recognising that 'people needed homes, not just houses' has led his name to be venerated by colleagues and competitors alike and almost immortalised by generations of discerning clients.

Born and bred in Ashton-under-Lyne - never one of the most fashionable mill towns that ring metropolitan Greater Manchester - this greengrocer's son, who went on to commute by helicopter, first took to the road that led from proverbial rags to riches on the saddle of a Lambretta scooter in the late 1950s.

Strapped to his back were timbers of freshly planed wood, meticulously prepared in advance for some small job of joinery work, won by a meld of keen pricing and disarming charm. Inevitably, a bag of tools was contained in the pannier. It says much of Roland Bardsley's feel for the call of destiny that the remittance advice for the very first payment he ever received - worth all of £9-0s-6d in old currency, from a now-defunct firm of mill furnishers, in March, 1959 - was kept, mounted and framed, on his office wall.

This talismanic memento represented the initial stepping-stone that would transform his prospects from time-served, if itinerant, carpenter to stewardship of a construction group that, by the close of the 20th Century, was turning over in excess of £60-million a year.

The Bardsley bandwagon began its roll in earnest in early 1962, when he took rooms above his father's greengrocery warehouse, in Camp Street, Ashton, as a makeshift builders yard to house the then embryonic firm of Roland Bardsley (Builders) Limited. The rent was £5 a week.

Within months expansion dictated a move, firstly to nearby Fleet Street, then onto Globe Square, Dukinfield - a prescient choice, since the location would develop and expand to become the headquarters of a group manned by 700 personnel and Ashton's biggest employer.

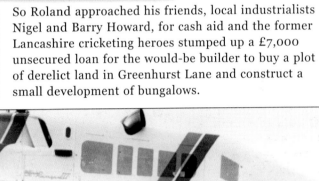

While the Sixties swung to the sound of The Beatles, flower-power ruled and George Best mesmerised crowds at nearby Old Trafford, Britain was basking in consumer confidence, a fact echoed by the seminal changes in people's attitude to where and how they lived. A housing boom was gaining momentum at an almost frantic pace - a fact that didn't go unnoticed by Roland Bardsley.

Creative, ambitious and imbued with the flair of a natural entrepreneur, he saw his opportunity and was determined to seize it with both hands. Only the perennial problem that besets most small businessmen - a lack of financial muscle - restrained him.

Above: Roland Bardsley with Gladys Smith, a local pensioner who fulfilled her ambition to fly in a helicopter courtesy of Roland. *Below:* Roland with his helicopter, 1990.

So Roland approached his friends, local industrialists Nigel and Barry Howard, for cash aid and the former Lancashire cricketing heroes stumped up a £7,000 unsecured loan for the would-be builder to buy a plot of derelict land in Greenhurst Lane and construct a small development of bungalows.

"I think everyone meets people, somewhere, who change the direction of their life," Roland recalled years later. "The Howard's generosity changed mine. They played cricket and hockey for England, flew their own, twin-engined plane and they seemed like god's to me."

Typically, no-one worked harder or longer to make Greenhurst Lane a success, albeit a minor one in the larger scale of things to come. But, significantly, the project helped Roland establish an ethos that both made his name and figuratively built his reputation.

He explained, "It made me realise the need to be involved, personally, in the design of every house, right down to the finest detail. So, when I walk down an avenue where we're building, and I don't like the look of it, I will have it changed."

Only a practised, natural eye, allied to an innate flair for style and design symmetry - some would call it 'taste' - could have been employed to such telling effects. Roland Bardsley had such gifts in abundance. And his commercial vision displayed similar virtuosity.

With the advent of the Seventies, Roland's instincts recognised a series of far-reaching business opportunities that others failed to see and in 1971 he moved to acquire Droylsden Racing & Equestrian Centre, in Sandy Lane, for the then not insignificant sum of £17,000. It was the home of Manchester's only American-style, trotting racetrack, where jockeys rode in lightweight jalopies, harnessed to the horses. Roland's ante, however, wasn't being placed on the nags, but on the ground they raced round - prime development acreage for future homes. The problem was it was deemed 'white', that is land without planning consent for redevelopment. Which was why expert opinion at the time regarded such a purchase as unwise. For Roland Bardsley's part, he ignored the advice, did the deal - and the land went on to be worth millions.

Further illustrations of that amazing foresight that spelt the difference between great business entrepreneurs and those that merely worked to live quickly followed. In 1975 Roland began to see the massive, evolving potential offered by the leisure industry and formed Bardo Electrics. Housed in Fitzroy Street, Droylsden, it was designed as a collect-and-repair service for pub equipment. A year later the name was changed to Bardsley Brewery Equipment Services Limited, which itself was destined to become Microflow (UK), then Microflow (Europe) Limited - and emerge as one of Britain's leading providers of high-tech, electronic beer delivery systems.

As with the housing boom of the Sixties, the Seventies was an era when the great British public found itself with time on its hands and a desire to enjoy itself. Leisure was the buzzword and people, growing evermore sophisticated, demanded high-class entertainment. Roland duly obliged with yet another departure from his core business of building homes. He opened Carriages Nightclub and Restaurant, in time for Christmas, 1975, as part of the Droylsden Racing & Equestrian Centre. The superb facilities featured a chic dinery, with international cuisine, overlooking the floodlit harness racing circuit, a

nightclub and seven bars, each of which was themed to commemorate travel and transport through the ages.

The club's main bar, for instance, replicated a barge in a canal tunnel, much to the delight and amusement of locals, all too familiar with the miles of man-made, Victorian waterways that criss-crossed Tameside. A stunningly instant hit, Carriage quickly became a mecca for lifestyle-conscious fun-seekers and Roland just as rapidly capitalised on its success - and the exploding popularity of the game of squash rackets - by extending the complex. Modifying the name to Carriages Leisure Centre, he built seven, championship-class squash courts, with stylish changing facilities, luxurious lounges and impressive conference rooms.

The Centre was formerly inaugurated by avid squash enthusiast and TV comedy icon, Leonard Rossiter - legendary star of The Fall & Rise of Reginald Perrin and later, the immortal Rigsby in Rising Damp - and former world squash champion, Geoff Hunt. By 1978 demand for the Carriages sports facilities was so high,

four further courts were created, making the centre the premier tournament venue in the North West.

With the advent of the Eighties, the burgeoning Bardsley group of companies were beginning to pass important performance milestones. These consolidated Roland's position as a respected businessman and brought the RB logo further into the public domain.

By 1982 turnover of Roland Bardsley (Builders) Limited broke the £10-million-a-year barrier. Three years later it exceeded £12-million - and for the first time the company sold over 100 homes in the space of a year. Under Roland's dynamic guidance and fuelled by his accomplished commercial acumen, each division - for that is what they had become - of the group soared ever onward and upward to fresh levels of performance. As profitability increased, more new jobs were created, more sites developed and - significantly -

Above: *One of the executive homes on the Coe Lane development at Tarleton.*

the Globe Square HQ, at Dukinfield, became an ever more vital hub for ideas and projects. However, little illustrated the man's consummate vision, tenacity and business bravura than the Droylsden Racing & Equestrian Centre project. Showing progress in every operational facet, the ultimate goal was reached in 1985 when planning consent was eventually given for residential development. Roland Bardsley's ambitious, £17,000 gamble - if, indeed, it could ever be considered a wager in the first place by a man blessed with astonishing foresight - of 14 years earlier was poised to reap handsome dividends.

This was achieved by Carriages, the operators of the Droylsden sport and leisure complex, selling off their prime land asset to corporate cousin, Roland Bardsley (Builders) Limited, who, in turn, drew up an attractive scheme to construct a tranche of new homes, exactly where a demanding public most wanted them.

Carriages, however, was also poised to make new acquisitions and in 1987 the group's first foray into the hospitality business began with the purchase of the Ruskin Hotel, in Albert Road, Blackpool. Within a year

Below: The Tabley House development, which the firm renovated and converted into superior dwellings in 1996.

- using the tried and tested Roland Bardsley ethos of delivering high value at affordable prices - demand for bookings at the Ruskin were running at such a brisk levels it was necessary to expand. Hence, in March, 1988, a deal was done with Britannia Hotels to acquire their adjacent property and merge the two into one.

As with all projects he undertook, Roland played a keynote and 'hands-on' role in developing the hotel. With a grant from the English Tourist Board, he practically rebuilt it from the inside out, creating 75 bedrooms - all with en-suite facilities - a new residents' restaurant, two function rooms and a public bar, aptly named Roly's.

With Roland Bardsley (Builders) turnover exceeding £30-million for the first time, he celebrated his success by acquiring a Bell Jet Ranger helicopter. To some it appeared an indulgence, but to Roland - ever pragmatic, always far seeing - it was a necessary tool of the trade. What better way could there be for him to evaluate land opportunities than from the air and facilitate his visits to his diverse operations.

As the building division, which now included a commercial contracting arm, grew into a £40-million-a-year undertaking by 1990, further consolidation had

taken place, with Microflow selling its Droylsden headquarters and relocating to purpose-built premises in Globe Square. In recognition of its accelerated expansion into the niche business as a supplier and manufacturer of beer dispense equipment, in 1995 the company name was changed again, this time to Microflow (Europe) Limited.

Meanwhile, the turnover of Roland Bardsley (Builders) continued remorselessly upward, with the £50-million mark achieved in 1995 and the company now firmly established as a major - respected and envied - player in the new-homes construction industry. A year on Roland's instinctive perception brought another jewel into the Bardsley crown. One of his favourite dining locations, The Swan Hotel, at Newby Bridge, Cumbria, where the waters of Lake Windermere fed the River Leven, came on the market, the family owners forsaking their interest in the 17th Century former coaching inn, with its 36 rooms, all of which were in need of some tender, loving refurbishment. Carriages Leisure acquired The Swan in November, 1996, and within a year had totally transformed it into Lakeland's premier, four-star, family hotel. The bedroom block, with its dated, Sixties facade, was swept away to be replaced by a handsome structure far more at one with a rural backdrop featuring some of England's finest scenery. Fifty-five, superb and tastefully appointed new bedrooms, plus six luxurious suites, were created, along with a leisure spa incorporating a magnificent swimming pool, gymnasium and sauna. Meanwhile, the original coaching house buildings - dating back to 1650 - were sympathetically restored to include new restaurant and bar areas. Needless to say, every intricate detail had to pass the critical scrutiny of Roland himself. "Only the very best will do," he would firmly insist. Similarly, further expansion of The Swan in Millennium Year, when the first-floor Orangery was created to provide extra facilities for functions and wedding receptions, equally bore the indelible imprimatur of Roland Bardsley on each facet.

With businesses turning over tens of millions, by 2001 some logistical restructuring was due and Roland took steps to create a series of more manageable, autonomous companies - Roland Bardsley Homes, Bardsley Construction and G.L. Joinery - each operating under the Group umbrella. Tragically, this was to be the final corporate act, because on April 1, 2001, the genius who rose from nowhere to the pinnacle of commercial greatness, passed away, aged 71. An intensely private man, unlike many of his high-achieving peers; Roland never craved the limelight, but chose to devote his spare time to his wife, Anne, sons, daughter, grandchildren and family.

Many of his countless kindnesses to others went unreported, but he was always eager to lend a helping hand, especially to those in his hometown of Ashton. Many local organisations benefited measurably from his financial support, but it was often the small, personal considerations - like giving a pensioner a 90th birthday present of a flight over her birthplace in his helicopter - Roland Bardsley relished most.

No monuments are necessary reminders of his remarkable life, because they are all around - the countless homes he built, the companies he created, the value-for-money business ethos he bequeathed to future generations. Those close to Roland Bardsley will remember him as one of the great Lancashire business entrepreneurs, a master builder who created a construction dynasty. They will equally recall a man with a zestful passion for life, a friend, colleague, leader and mentor, who unfailingly rewarded loyalty with unswerving dedication.

Above: Roland and his wife, Anne.

Safe from northern weather

'What's the weather going to be like?' Ask that question in our part of the world and the answer is likely to be 'Pass'. Four seasons in a day isn't uncommon in Lancashire and once you get up onto those Pennine hills four seasons in an hour is more often the case.

But unpredictable weather is not something that puts us off packing sandwiches and pulling on hiking boots, fleeces and waterproofs.

Mancunians may live in a city but it's a city where the countryside is never far away. For generations the city's residents have been getting away from traffic and mill chimneys fumes to stretch their legs and fill their lungs with country air. But the down-side has always

been the risk of getting soaked to the skin in the process.

Our parents and grandparents covered themselves up with mackintoshes and plastic pixie hoods, but these days hill walkers are blessed with a wide variety of

Right: *Joanne, Lionel and Keith Black.*
Below: *Celebrating the re-opening of the Lake District following the disastrous Foot and Mouth epidemic in 2001.*

purpose made, lightweight fashionable walking clothes. And one local firm above all has been responsible for that revolution in outdoor clothing .

Regatta Ltd was originally called Risol the name being taken from the first names of Risol's owner, businessman Solly Krauz, and his wife Rita. The company was based in Manchester and originally sold wholesale protective clothing to local industry from the back of a van.

Solly was an astute businessman, good at buying and selling profitably; he soon identified great sales opportunities and Risol developed into a fine business buying industrial footwear and fell boots from Spain and Romania and selling them to Army and Navy surplus stores.

By the time Risol was sold to the Black family in 1977 there were six employees and the company had an annual turnover of £1 million. When Solly sold the business he emigrated to Israel but later returned to England and worked as Regatta's sales rep for London until he retired in the mid 1990s.

Helpfully Harold Kahan, who had worked with Solly for six years, stayed with the company as Sales Manager and would become Sales Director. Nat Weisz the Accounts Manager would also stay to help the new owners.

The Black family had been making waterproofs for over 70 years. Lionel Black took over his family rainwear business, the Benson Black Waterproofs Company, and when he left the army in 1945 changed the company's name to Dhobi. That business thrived during the 1950s and was floated on the stock market in the next decade becoming a household name. In 1968 however Dhobi was taken over by a large conglomerate and, though Lionel Black stayed for several years, in 1977 he left and bought Risol from Solly Krauz.

Having taken over Risol the first major development was that Lionel Black moved from dealing with

Above: The award winning Stormbreak jacket.

importers to actually being an importer; in 1979 he became one of the first British businessmen to venture into China.

The first major coup for the company was buying cotton bags in assorted colours and styles from central China. During those early visits to China Lionel Black and his son, Keith, were often the first westerners the local people had ever seen.

In 1982 Risol received a delivery of fashionable see-through waterproof jackets from Taiwan with a Regatta label and a picture of a boat, the garments were originally intended for a German company. The jackets went down a storm, the name stuck and a new brand name, Regatta, was born.

Other major successes at this time included selling Italian army clothing which was made popular through the endorsement of a pop group as well as the fashionable Manchester Parka with its navy outer and orange lining.

In 1984 Risol became the first UK company to buy quality waterproof clothing from China. Three years later the Regatta waterproof Stormbreak jacket received a Best Buy accolade in the Which Report. The Which award marked the beginning of Regatta's rise to national brand status. This style consistently won Regatta similar awards and would go on to sell no fewer than 3 million by 2002.

The introduction of Isotex a breathable waterproof fabric in 1989 was also instrumental in establishing the company as a major player in the outdoor clothing market. It became the first outdoor clothing company to develop a waterproof and breathable jacket at an affordable price despite the complicated manufacturing process: fabric was bought in Asia, shipped to the UK to be treated with a waterproof and breathable coating then shipped back to Asia to be made up into jackets before being shipped back to the UK to be sold!

In 1995 the company was renamed Regatta and a conscious effort was made to focus on the outdoor clothing and equipment markets and develop the Regatta name. Risol now became the holding company for Regatta.

retail at Burtons and Hobbs then joined the company in 1989 to become, in due course, Group Buying Director with specific responsibly for 'Craghoppers' as well as overseeing eight factory retail outlets located across the country.

That was however still in the future. From 1991 onwards, the company began a major marketing programme including national advertising to develop Regatta as a national household brand. It was also at this time that a design team and facilities were developed to further evolve the range which until then had been designed personally by Harold Kahan and Lionel and Keith Black; often reserving Sunday mornings for this crucial task.

In 1995 the Craghoppers brand was bought; originally launched as a hill walking brand Craghoppers and its range of clothing and equipment for men and women, would quickly develop into a leading active outdoor and travel brand. The same year a Regatta shop was opened in Fleetwood.

As the company grew new premises were required and in a short space of time the company went from Chadderton to Rochdale then in 1983 it moved to its current premises at Risol House in Urmston. It was also at this stage that agents were introduced to help actively increase sales.

The Regatta offices are unpretentious and down to earth. This is not a business obsessed with prestige and looking good from the outside; it's what's inside that counts.

As a family proud of its business it was a natural progression for Keith and Joanne, Lionel Black's son and daughter, to join the company. Keith joined in 1981 after having studied law at university; he now holds the position of Managing Director. Joanne studied business at university before gaining experience in

Top left: Regatta's premises, Risol House in Urmston. **Right:** *Regatta imagery from the Spring/Summer 2003 photo shoot.*

Regatta is an unashamedly family business. The Blacks consider the company as an extension of the family. People are very important to them and as well as pursuing conventional personnel development programmes such as Investors in People the family genuinely care for staff and find ways to enable them to grow within the business, in turn making them partners in leadership. Many staff have been with the company for decades.

That stable workforce would have a direct impact on the quality of Regatta's products. The company's staff includes many passionate outdoor enthusiasts who wear the company's gear and regularly offer solutions and suggestions for new product ideas.

And those who wanted to buy Regattas products were finding it ever easier to do so. In 1999 Regatta factory shops opened in Castleford in Yorkshire and in Braintree, Essex.

There was more development in the pipeline too. In 2000 Regatta launched Dare2be - a snow-wear brand with European appeal with ranges for men, women and children. In 2001 three more factory shops opened in Swindon, Livingston and Hornsea.

Today the Regatta Group exports to over 22 countries with dedicated sales offices in France, Germany and Holland. Products are distributed from Regatta's two warehouses which cover 30,000 sq. meters - equivalent to eight football pitches.

In the opening years of the new century Lionel Black's passion to create the best possible products at the lowest possible price still extends to ensuring that overheads are kept to a minimum: at the age of 80 he is still walking the corridors of the company turning off the lights in empty rooms.

Lionel Black never thought that Regatta would grow to the size it would become; but with 300 employees, four dedicated offices across Europe and a turnover in excess of £50 million the company is now a remarkable testament to his hard work and entrepreneurial spirit.

Top left: Regatta's Spring/summer 2002 advertising campaign.
Left: The main entrance to Risol House.

Keeping cool

There was a time not too long ago when air conditioning meant opening a window when it was too hot and closing it again when it got too cool. Well, maybe that is being a little too simplistic; in fact Romans introduced under-floor central heating to our part of the world almost two thousand years ago, whilst if we wanted to get really cool ice houses were around long before electric refrigerators made their first appearance. In the 18th century the wealthy would even have ice houses sunk deep in the earth in the grounds of their mansions; servants would hack ice from nearby lakes in winter and pack it in sawdust to be stored underground until it was called for in the summer months. In the USA that same principle would later be applied on an industrial scale, with ice from the Great Lakes being cut, stored and delivered by train to cities all over the USA. When the electric refrigerator was first invented a similar method of distribution was initiated with ice being produced by huge refrigerators and blocks of ice delivered to individual customers who would store their ice block in an insulated ice-box.

Now in the 21st century however opening a window to get cool or putting more coal on the fire to get warm, let alone having a block of ice delivered to the door is a thing of the past. Central heating in ordinary homes has been commonplace since the 1960s, though until recently similar systems also keep us cool in summer, something more usually associated with the USA than with Lancashire, have been relative strangers to these parts. Air conditioning though has been gaining ground in recent years, and even if it is not something we tend to find much of a need for in our homes, it is becoming an increasingly common feature in our larger public buildings, hotels and office blocks.

One of the most important firms responsible for introducing Britain to air-conditioning is Manchester's very own Temperature Control Ltd based in Old Trafford. And although Temperature Control is a provider of some of the most up to date products imaginable its history goes back more than a century.

Top left: Company founder, Mr E O Walker. *Above right:* Mr H P Walker who took over the running of the firm in 1942. *Right:* The interior of the first premises. *Below:* An early delivery vehicle.

The firm was founded by a Mr EO Walker in 1898 who provided moving pictures on a projector screen which he carried round to large houses and to any other building that had electricity at that time. EO Walker had immediately grasped the commercial opportunities of the new silent movie industry.

Electricity was the wonder of the age at the turn of the century. Today we take electricity for granted and forget that, just within living memory, it was very much a novelty. Though electricity had been known of and experimented with for many decades it was not of much practical use. Electricity seeped into most peoples lives only by degrees: first the electric telegraph followed by the telephone. Mass familiarity with electricity came however with the electric trams.

But what to use the new electricity for at home? There was no TV, no radio, no domestic fridges nor power tools. The answer was light. The electric light bulb had been invented by Swann and Edison towards the end of the 19th century and now everyone was clamouring to switch from gas mantles to the far superior electric lighting.

An electrical shop was opened in Cannon Street by EO Walker in 1926.

The founder was followed in the business by his son HP Walker who took over from him in 1942. Very little is known about HP Walker other than that he continued to run the firm as an electrical retail shop. The firm sold light fittings and later began to sell refrigerators, becoming one of the first companies in the country to obtain a Kelvinator franchise. Sadly the firm's progress not only halted but now went into decline with far fewer employees on the books when HP Walker finished than when he had taken over in 1942. After 20 years the business only had some half dozen staff employees.

The firm was sold in the early 1960s to Mr W Latta who continued to run the business as a refrigeration firm under the name of EO Walker Refrigeration Ltd and began to specialise in supplying shops with refrigeration units.

Commercial refrigerated display units were just beginning to become popular at this time. Though refrigerated storage in warehouses had been commonplace for years this was something which was just starting to make its way into shops more widely.

Top: Mr W Latta who bought the firm in the early 1960s. *Left:* The Queen visiting Walker's stand at an exhibition. *Below:* An early shop refrigerator.

Frozen food was coming to be more widely available and names like Birdseye and Findus were becoming household names for their frozen food which was not only kept in home freezers but was now sold even in corner shops. And not just corner shops, in the early 1960s supermarkets were just beginning their rise to market dominance. Large fridges were common enough in butchers' shops and fish mongers but until now goods had been kept cool for display by putting them out on marble slabs with a generous dollop of crushed ice. Now with ever improving fridge technology, allied with improved materials, such as plastics, whole displays could be refrigerated.

These days when we have got used to the sight of rank upon rank of cabinet fridges in our supermarkets we have almost forgotten what it was like to buy food that was cool rather than frozen as it is now. The wire mesh meat safe has been consigned to history as much as saw dust liberally spread over the floor of butchers" shops.

Before buying out EO Walker Mr Latta had been managing Director of Simons Foods in Newton-le-Willows. After buying the business the firm moved to Walker House in Chorlton Street, Old Trafford, and also moved into air conditioning.

During the 1970s the company's activities in supplying

refrigerated display units diminished as the company concentrated on process cooling, cold rooms and on the relatively new market for the installation of commercial air conditioning. By the early 1980s the commercial air conditioning market had grown rapidly and had become the mainstay of the business.

In 1983 the company name was changed from EO Walker Refrigeration to Temperature Control Ltd to reflect the change of focus into air conditioning.

In the early years air conditioning had been hard to get off the ground. Fortunately the company had joined the air conditioning market very early on and was poised and ready when it did eventually take off. Temperature Control quickly became involved with the

Top left: *Some staff members in the 1970s.*
Top right: *The firm's premises on Chorlton Street, Old Trafford, Manchester in the 1970s.* **Above:** *Tom White with one of the firm's new vans in 1970.* **Left:** *The first 'custom built' industrial system.*

introduction of VRF systems in the late 1980s and by the early 1990s it was rapidly becoming one of the country's premier specialist VRF air conditioning contractors.

Staff are trained in installing equipment from the four major air conditioning suppliers: Hitachi, Mitsubishi, Daikin and Toshiba and are approved installers for each of them; however the company has no particular allegiance to any one manufacturer and can therefore select the product most suitable for any particular site.

All the air conditioning units sold are heat pumps to provide a coefficient of performance of 400 per cent, a feature which greatly reduces running costs in the colder months with the added bonus of cooling in the summer.

To date Temperature Control has installed air conditioning in all the malls and some of the larger stores in the Trafford Centre, the Mal Maison Hotel in Manchester and even the laser cooling system on top of Blackpool Tower. Customers include main banks, building societies and large hotels. Sales are made throughout the UK from offices in, not only Manchester, but also Birmingham, Cardiff and London and the company has been involved in projects across the globe.

The business has carried out installations throughout the UK and Eire and has also built plant for container-

isation and delivery to Holland, Switzerland, Italy, Indonesia, Mexico, Canada and the Ascension Islands.

With more than 30 staff Temperature Control Ltd is one of the largest specialist air conditioning contractors in Britain with an annual turnover of more than £8 million. The company's fully qualified design teams offer full design services where required as part of design and build projects and are experienced in a wide range of commercial, industrial and retail applications.

Today Temperature Control Ltd's aim is to provide the highest quality air conditioning installation selected specifically to satisfy its customers' requirements whilst offering maximum cost effectiveness.

Top right: Modern refrigerated units in a shop. Left: Air-conditioned office premises. Below: Replacing old water cooling towers at a local hospital.

Solid steel

The business known today as Austin Trumanns was founded by two men named Fletcher and Livingstone; the firm began in 1948 as the Eiffel Foundry which at that time manufactured iron castings and was located just yards away from the firm's current site in Moss Lane, Walkden. Employing just 36 staff the business would become the largest jobbing foundry in the North West producing castings of up to 30 tons mainly for the machine tool industry.

With the advent of steel fabrications foundries went into decline and the Eiffel Foundry, anticipating the long term impact, moved into steel stockholding.

Steel was in great demand during the 1960s due to all the rebuilding after the second world war though availability was very tight and steel was sold under licence.

Most stockholders were old established family firms and competitive prices and a quick reliable delivery service was unheard of: normal delivery lead times were 4 to 5 days for stock material sold off a standard price list.

The name Trumanns appeared in the 1960s when John Fletcher was searching for a new name for the company. At the time cricketer Freddie Trueman was in fine batting form whilst brewers Watney Mann was bidding for the

Truman's brewery. The fine sounding name Trumanns Steel somehow emerged from these events.

Trumanns' foundations were built on competitive prices and quick reliable delivery. The company published its first independent price list in 1967 undercutting the industry's standard price lists. As a result sales grew significantly over the next six years.

In 1975 John Fletcher retired and his son, also John Fletcher, took over. The steel stockholding industry changed significantly in the 1970s. Large national groups were formed with companies such as British Steel buying up many old established family firms.

The Trumanns Steel Group was now formed as a successor to the original business though remaining an independent steel stockholder.

In 1983 a successful bid was made for James Austin & Sons Ltd a Yorkshire business established in 1850 and based in

*Top left: Company founder, John Fletcher. **Above right:** The founder's son, also called John, who was Managing Director until 1997.*
***Right:** Stores of steel girders from the early years.*

Dewsbury. The acquisition doubled turnover and broadened the product range and the geographical range of sales.

The mid to late 1980s saw steady growth and good economic conditions. In 1985 the company was renamed Austin Trumanns bringing together the names of the two firms.

The acquisition of Chilko Ltd in 1987 saw a move into strip products; an investment programme increased Chilko's capacity eightfold at its factories in St Helens, Knutsford and Manchester.

Meanwhile steel sales continued to grow and in 1988 a sales office was opened near Wolverhampton. A warehouse was also

bought and a Midlands division began trading in 1990. John Fletcher died in 1994 and in 1997 John Fletcher junior sold his remaining shares to Murray International Holdings Ltd, a company which had held an interest in the company for many years. Austin Trumanns now moved towards the next century as part of the Murray Metals Group within MIH, a company with interests world-wide which included metals, property, mining, sports and marketing. As a result of these changes the company became part of the largest independent steel stockholder in the UK.

A very competitive steel market in the late 1990s however has lead to a significant refocusing of the business. Austin Trumanns returned to its roots in general steels whilst scaling down its activity in strip products and rebranding itself with a new logo and newly liveried vehicles.

In early 1999 due to restructuring of the group's core activities a profiling service began in new premises in Brighouse, West Yorkshire.

As the world moved into a new millennium Austin Trumanns opened a purpose-built facility in Newry, Northern Ireland providing state of the art warehousing capacity servicing the whole of Ireland.

Today Austin Trumanns provides a truly national delivery network operating in Lancashire, Yorkshire, the West Midlands, the West Country, the North East, Scotland and Ireland whilst retaining its traditional approachability and local expertise.

Not only does the group offer a huge range of general steels from the smallest rounds, flats, squares and angles it also supplies the largest universal beams and columns along with a vast range of steel plates, sheets and hollow sections, most of which have gone into notable and high profile construction projects.

Top left: Major redevelopment of the Head Office at Walkden. Above left: The firm's current Managing Director, Graeme Hill. Left: Loading one of the many delivery low-loaders. Below: Austin Trumann's Walkden facility pictured in 2001.

Pack up your troubles

When something is so commonplace, like buses or electricity, it is only when they are not there that we are reminded of how important they are. Packaging is rather like that. We are usually so concerned with the inside of a package that we rarely take much interest in the outer covering which has served its vital duty protecting the contents during the time since the goods left the factory. But without good packaging we'd experience some terrible problems.

Packaging Products Ltd has occupied the same site at the Little Green Works in Collyhurst Road, Collyhurst since 1841. In that year Henry Leicester, a local builders merchant, formed a company to manufacture tarpaulin and oiled cloth for packaging.

Collyhurst, which means a hill dirty with coal dust, probably obtained its name from the burning of charcoal, because, during the middle ages, the area was famous for its oak woods.

Sandstone outcrops occur in the area and the Romans used this sandstone to build the fort wall at Castlefield and Deansgate. The same sandstone was later used to build the city cathedral. This area, being one mile from the city centre and situated on the River Irk meant that it was developed with factories on each bend of the river during the 18th century as well as terraced housing for the workers.

Top left: *John Blackwell in his role as Mayor of Hyde, 1904/5.* **Above:** *An artists impression of the mill in 1888.*

In 1853 one of Henry's relatives, 12 year old John Blackwell, joined him. At first John was paid just half a crown (12.5p) for working up to 80 hours a week before being put in charge of the business in the 1860s. Henry Leicester allowed young John to start up his own business whilst still working for him and in 1873, at the age of 33, John took over Henry's business and merged it with his own to form John Blackwell & Sons.

In 1884 the new company took out a patent for the machine production of cotton bale wrapping - material which had previously been made by hand - the new machine would draw cloth by power through an oil trough during the process of making oil cloth which not only increased production speed but also improved the uniformity of the product.

John Blackwell would become an important figure in the local community; in 1895 he was elected to Hyde Council for Werneth Ward and would subsequently be re-elected in 1898 and 1902. In 1903 he was elected to the Aldermen's bench and in 1904, this now patriarchal bearded figure, became mayor.

In 1897 John's son, John Duncan Blackwell, took out a patent in his own name for an improved cotton bale wrap, designed to keep exported cotton goods packed in bales free from water penetration during their long voyages to export markets around the world. The patent application document is an interesting one since it makes clear that the oil cloth previously used for this purpose, commonly based on linen, had a tendency to become brittle and crack as well as being unduly heavy. The new patent oil cloth would have as its base plain cotton cloth made of a specially heavy yarn impregnated with a waterproof composition made up of two parts cotton seed pitch to one part of stearine pitch. That 'patent wrap' was still being sold in the UK up until the 1970s, its demise coinciding with the demise of the UK's cotton industry.

In 1900 John Blackwell & Sons amalgamated with eight other small packaging companies to form Packaging Materials Association Ltd - 'PMA' - with John Blackwell as Chairman.

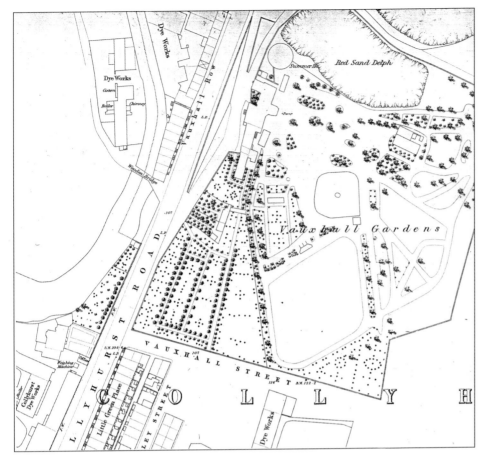

The firm now passed to the chairmanship of William's son Alan. On the outbreak of war in 1939 the company supplied packaging materials to the army - part of the armed services in which could be found Alan's younger brother Donald. Because of its strategic importance to the war effort half the firm's production was now moved to Hadfield for greater safety whilst the vacated space was used for storage by the War Office. PPL supply packaging material to the MoD to this day.

Following the war PMA(Holdings) Ltd formed Packaging Products (Holdings) Ltd which in turn started to diversify with the acquisition of a waxing company Koters of Liverpool and Superior Packaging in Ireland.

PMA had changed its own name to Packaging Products Ltd in 1957 by which time John Blackwell had succeeded his father Alan whilst his uncle Donald worked as the company's Sales Director.

By 1965 Packaging Products (Holdings) Ltd would own several subsidiary companies: Packaging Products Ltd; Koters (Liverpool) Ltd; Superior Coaters Ltd; Vitaloid Products (Manchester) Ltd; Flexothene Ltd and Vitaloid Products Ltd in addition to Superior Coaters' own subsidiaries: Superior Packaging Products Ltd and Presson Labels Ltd.

In his later years John Blackwell moved to Southport; and following his death, in 1923, a beautiful stained glass window was dedicated to his memory at the Southbank Road Wesleyan church. Following John's death his son, Duncan, became chairman of the company - which would soon become wholly owned by the Blackwell family.

The original 17th century Little Green Works 100 yards from the present building had burned down in 1922. During the 19th century the original building was notable for being the oldest factory in Manchester.

Duncan's brother William Blackwell became chairman of the company following his brother's death at his home in the Isle of Man in 1927. William however would be chairman for only eight years before succumbing to a heart attack whilst travelling by train from his summer home on the Kyle of Bute to visit a customer in Glasgow.

Top left: A map dated 1848, showing the Collyhurst site on the left. On the opposite side of the road to Little Green Works can be seen Vauxhall Gardens which contained formal gardens, a bandstand and a mock castle.
Right: An application for the patent of the firm's waterproof cloth from 1897.

One of the group's acquisitions had been Turtle Wax, a brand much sought after by many larger businesses. After a complex series of deals Packaging Products Ltd now became jointly owned by PMA Holdings, Lloyd's Packaging Warehouses and Capseals.

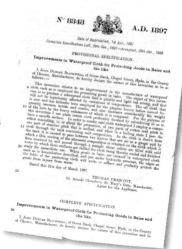

The three companies shared control, each supplying chairmen on a rotating basis. In 1967 however Capseals Ltd acquired full control and John Blackwell resigned as Managing Director ending over a century of Blackwells at the helm.

The last member of the Blackwell family to work for the firm, Donald, left the company in 1976 in the midst of a decade which saw the number of employees peak at 320.

In the early 1970s Capseals had decided that the diversification that had taken place with the movement into polythene film production, corrugated sheet plant production, gummed tape production, crepe paper production, tube winding manufacture and sales of paper and tapes were to be closed down, with both Koters and Superior to be sold, as the company concentrated on its core business of industrial wrappings.

At the same time the introduction of PE coated papers and film was superseding bitumen laminated papers and wax papers for use as waterproof wrappers. The bitumen and wax products had reached their zenith though the company was then producing 12,000 tonnes each year. The new strategy meant that time, effort and money could be found to introduce a successor to bitumen laminations and in 1972 a newly-patented method for coating paper was introduced: Blond Union, a hot melt water barrier.

During the 1970s acquisitions to add to the core business took place such as the purchase of Neptune, Brookgate and other smaller companies.

In 1981 the company acquired its largest UK competitor James

*Above: Duncan S Blackwell, pictured during the second world war. **Below:** The creping machine which was dismantled in 1971.*

world-wide. The firm had also received ISO 9002 approval in 1994.

In keeping with modern thinking Packaging Products introduced its own environmental policy aimed at producing new recyclable products to replace the old environmentally poor bitumen and wax products, minimising packaging weights and reducing energy usage. The company replaced its older hot-melt laminations with new cold-applied coatings and laminations to manufacture a product which would be totally recyclable. The company has spent ten years developing these products and building machines to manufacture them.

With its dedicated workforce, some of whom are the third generation of local families to work for the firm, the Company today is ready to face the 21st century; it looks forward to the current family in the business achieving the same success that was enjoyed for so long by the founding Blackwell family.

Above left and top left: Machines built by the company using the new patented coating method. Both machines are capable of speeds of 400 metres per minute.
Below: An aerial view of the site.

Barnes, which was based on Derby Street off Cheetham Hill, making it now the largest manufacturer of waterproof papers in Europe. In 1982 Packaging Products was sold by Capseals to Worcester Engineering, then a private company. Now old unprofitable lines were dropped and older buildings on the site demolished.

Retrenchment by Worcester Engineering, now known as Worcester Bosch, in the early 1990s however led to a management buy out led by John Cornford, the Managing Director since 1984.

In 1992 John Cornford became chairman whilst his son, Andrew, became Sales Director. Andrew's younger brother, Robert Cornford, joined the board as Production Director in 2000.

By the start of the new century the Company would be exporting more than 15 per cent of its sales to places as far away as Australasia, the Middle East as well as the EU countries; it had also received approval for a new product for use by the Toyota car company both in Japan and

Fired with enthusiasm

Which company is the fastest growing wholesaler in the country? The answer it turns out is Manchester's Stax Trade Centre Ltd based in Holloway Drive on the Wardley Industrial Estate in Worsley. Stax is a non-food, cash and carry wholesaler strictly for the trade and specialises in DIY, hardware and gardening products. Customers are mainly independent retailers. Between 1988 and the start of the new century Stax would treble the number of its branches and more than quadruple its turnover underlining its claim to be the most rapidly growing wholesaler in the country. But where did this extraordinarily dynamic company have its origins?

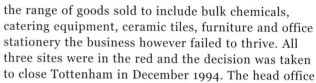

It was in 1981 that Stax Manchester began trading. By 1985 turnover had topped £4 million. The following year Eddie Brady and David Hibbert acquired the business from Maccess in a management buy-out.

That may sound simple, but things were rather more complicated than that. The original Stax Trade Centre goes back to a cash and carry wholesale business set up by Maccess the motor parts distributor back in 1981. Two Stax sites, Manchester and Leeds, opened that year.

Another branch opened in Tottenham, North London, in 1983. Despite increasing

*Top centre: From left to right; David Shore and Ken Widdowson of Maccess receive the final payment from Eddie Brady and David Hibbert in 1987. **Right:** A view of the interior of Stax, Manchester on the occasion of it's opening in 1981. **Below:** David Hibbert and Eddie Brady.*

the range of goods sold to include bulk chemicals, catering equipment, ceramic tiles, furniture and office stationery the business however failed to thrive. All three sites were in the red and the decision was taken to close Tottenham in December 1994. The head office in Leeds was also closed leaving just two branches, each with a high degree of autonomy.

The Manchester branch was left to be run by Eddie Brady who had been the branch manager there since its opening in 1981. In 1984, on the closure of the Tottenham branch and subsequently the Leeds office, David Hibbert was transferred to Manchester to work with Eddie with the responsibility for negotiating business terms and marketing.

Under Eddie and David the Manchester branch began to flourish as they exercised their autonomy, pioneering what would become the well known Stax formula of keen pricing and regular promotions on a comprehensive range of products stocked in depth.

Managing Director had to take out second mortgages on their homes to help finance the project. That year however Stax had moved into profit. Over two years sales increased at an annual average rate of 25 per cent to reach £4.2 million - and a £250,000 loss in 1984 was transformed into a healthy profit in 1986.

Everything seemed to be going well until, in September 1987, exactly a year after the management buy out, disaster struck and the premises burned to the ground.

In the early hours of the morning of September 18th a fire started at the site which rapidly grew into a blaze. Within the space of a couple of hours the blaze was an inferno. By the time the fire brigade had been alerted by local residents and arrived the roller shutter doors to the site were white hot.

Within 30 minutes of the fire brigade being on the scene the overhead power lines melted and had fallen onto nearby houses; this forced the firemen to withdraw until the power could be cut giving the fire even more time to take hold. By the time Eddie Brady and David Hibbert arrived most of the business was engulfed and they had to watch as their new venture went up in flames.

Surveying the wreckage the next day both David and Eddie were devastated by the smoking ruin of their business. However, once they had rid themselves of the flock of loss adjusters touting for business, the pair set about rebuilding their company. Fortunately a warehouse on the same industrial estate, though only two thirds of the size

Despite that triumph in Manchester however the Leeds branch continued to lose money. Maccess took the decision to close the Leeds branch and Eddie and David took the chance to buy out the Manchester branch.

The first suggestion of a management buy out had been mooted in 1985 but was given added impetus when Maccess itself was subject to a management buyout from Burmah Oil for £10.5 million. One month later, in September 1986, Eddie and David, helped financially by non-executive director Graham Gardiner, negotiated a £750,000 buy out from Maccess which resulted in the formation of Stax Trade Centres Ltd.

It was a big gamble. Both Eddie, who now became Chairman and joint Managing Director and David his co-

Top: Stax, Manchester as it looked in the early 1980s.
Above left: Ken Dodd with Eddie Brady, at the official opening of Stax, Manchester in 1981.

as the one destroyed, was vacant and they were able to move the business into it.

Stax tills started to ring again on 22nd November 1987, just nine weeks from the date of the fire.

While trading continued from the temporary site construction work began on a new building. In January 1988 the foundations of the new Manchester store were laid and nine months later Stax Manchester reopened - exactly a year to the day of the fire.

That same year Stax was able to open a Birmingham depot at Smethwick in the west Midlands. Within 12 months sales would top £10 million.

Having seen the original Leeds branch close in the 1980s Eddie and David now opened a new Leeds branch in 1992. Stax would go on to acquire its close rival WE Merris in Birmingham in 1995 and the following year the 52,000 sq ft Bristol branch of Stax would open.

Meanwhile back in the North West, in November 1996, Manchester was the first Stax branch to take over £100,000 in a single day.

In 1997 Stax rescued Liverpool based Domcraft Ltd from the receiver and re-launched Dompak-Grosvenor Ltd as a subsidiary company part of the Stax plc Group now based in Widnes and a wholesaler which delivers goods to customers rather than on a cash and carry basis.

In Manchester business continued to grow and in March 1997 the footings were laid for a new extension; by the

Top and inset: *The aftermath of the devastating fire that occurred in 1988.* ***Above:*** *Stax Trade Centre following refurbishment after the fire.*

Liverpool to new premises in Widnes. From a turnover of £2.5 million in 1981 sales had grown every single year, slowly at first reaching just £15 million in 1991 before rapidly taking off to reach that staggering £70 million at the start of the new millennium.

And it was not just sales that had grown. In the years since its founding staff numbers had increased from 50 to over 600. In 1987 the wages bill was £380,000, by 2000 it had reached £7.6 million. Staff who joined the firm as general assistants on the shop floor could, with hard work and commitment, become senior managers within the group. Four members of staff who were with the company from its foundation and would witness all its spectacular growth are Della Butler, Lynda Brooks, Sue Hoben and Phil Hand.

The growth of Stax has been remarkable, however nothing would have been possible without Eddie Brady and David Hibbert who bravely risked their all back in 1986.

end of August that year the new look Manchester was opened despite the challenge of floods in the Timber & Building section, burst pipes in the car park which meant no water for the kitchen and toilets and staff having to troop down the road to use other facilities and, for a while, no gas or heating. One million pounds was invested in the extension, increasing space by over a third. Not only did Stax have to buy out its next door neighbour but, because the site was some 18 feet higher than the existing store, the removal of the excess land alone would cost over £160,00 for the excavations in order to add an extra 14,000 sq ft to the existing 38,000 sq ft warehouse.

Expansion continued elsewhere too. Stax bought the Woodside brand in 1998. By 1999 turnover topped £59 million helped by opening on Saturdays for the first time.

In the year 2000 Stax launched its Supavalue range and Stax websites. Stax also made the headlines when in April of that year some of the company's staff came face to face with masked robbers who had entered the building, but being confronted by courageous staff the robbers had to flee empty handed.

In 2001 a new Birmingham depot opened and turnover reached £70 million whilst Dompak moved from

*Top left: An aerial view of Stax, Manchester following the extension in 1997. **Above left and below:** Graham Gardiner opening the Bristol branch in 1996, left, and David Hibbert and Eddie Brady with Sharon Davies on the same occasion, below.*

Donns Solicitors - a legal eagle

Raymond Donn, the founder of Donns Solicitors, was born on 17th March 1944 the eldest son of a prominent local community figurehead in the North West, Leslie Donn JP, a former Chairman of Whitefield UDC and Chairman of Bury Magistrates. Determined to follow the ambition of his father Raymond Donn founded his legal practice in 1969 as Donn & Co with a firm commitment to service. Today the once small firm is one of the largest in the country specialising in the area of Personal Injury.

The firm of Donn & Co started out from offices at 26 Cross Street, Manchester and stayed there until April 1997 when, due to expansion, it moved to 201 Deansgate.

At varying times before moving to Deansgate however the firm also had a number of offices around Manchester including ones in Blackley, Moston, Droylsden, Openshaw, Withington, Walkden and Irlams O'Th' Height.

Initially Donn & Co offered a full range of typical legal services such as conveyancing, divorce, wills, personal injury and clinical negligence.

The firm quickly won a reputation for itself, though not always in expected ways. In 1972, when the Arndale Centre was being built, one of Raymond Donn's clients had taken a lease of a shop and was using non-union labour on the site. This was permitted under the terms of the agreement, however the unions did not like it and started picketing the site and threatening Raymond and his client. The unions even picketed outside Donn & Co's offices in Cross Street. Donn & Co promptly responded by obtaining injunc-

Top left: Raymond Donn pictured in 1969, the year he founded his firm. **Right:** *An early Donn & Co business card.*

tions against the union and its members - the court ordered them to stop picketing and threatened them with imprisonment. As a result the union called all its labour off the site and work on the Arndale development ground to a halt! Detailed discussion followed which resulted in a financial settlement to Donn & Co's client before normal service on the building site was resumed.

By the early 1990s the firm also had an office in Cambridge. This was a groundbreaking move for solicitors since it was the first solicitors' office to open in an NHS hospital. Donn & Co was also the first solicitors to advertise on the radio once the legal professions restrictions were relaxed to permit them to advertise.

Subsequently Donn & Co changed its name to become 'Donns Solicitors', at the same time the firm took the strategic decision to specialise purely in personal injury and to aim to become one of Britain's leading personal injury law practices.

That aim would be fulfilled. Just three years after its relocation to Deansgate Donns moved once again, this time to The Observatory, Chapel Walk after the firm had tripled in size in 24 months.

By the millennium Raymond Donn would be Senior Partner in what had become a very large firm indeed as well as being a Vice President of Manchester City Football Club.

Donns Solicitors had become one of the largest personal injury firms in the country. The firm now had 11 partners and over 300 dedicated staff with the highest proportion of female partners of any law firm in the United Kingdom.

And forget the dusty fusty image of a solicitors office, Donns was at the cutting edge of modernity. In July 2000

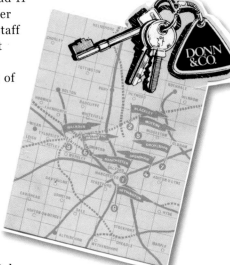

Donns became the first legal firm to offer individual clients and their insurance companies access to their files via the Internet using Donns' unique and innovative e-file-access facility. In December 2000 Donns Solicitors would win the insurance industry's 'Technology Innovation of the Year Award' for its e-file access system.

More spectacular progress was to follow. 2001 was a phenomenal year. The firm experienced a period of exceptional growth and was the only firm of solicitors to be ranked in the Inner City 100 Index. Donns was ranked 64th in the index which recognised the fastest growing companies within the UK.

That same year Donns also secured the Duke of Westminster Award, the North West's most prestigious award recognising business excellence. And that award was only the start: Donns was then awarded Lexcel accreditation, the Law Society's own quality award for practice management and Investors in People accreditation for its dedication to staff development and training.

Following the success of Donns' unique e-file-access in winning the Technology Innovation of the Year Award at the Insurance Industry Awards the system went on to win the Computer Weekly E-business Excellence Award for Customer Relationship Management in 2001. Donns was still the only firm able to offer the e-file-access facility to clients.

Meanwhile there was some spectacular legal work being done too. For example Managing Partner, Hilary

Top: Receiving the Technology Innovation of the Year Award at the Insurance Industry Awards in 2000.
Above left: *Hilary and Raymond receiving the Duke of Westminster Award for business excellence in 2001 from the Duke.*

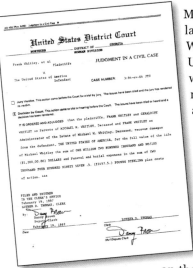

Meredith, won a landmark case - Whitley and Others v US Government - with some $12 million being awarded on appeal.

In 2001 alone Donns recovered more than £55 million in damages for clients and had a record breaking year for fees, up almost 24 per cent on the previous year.

Donns' specialist Uninsured Loss Recovery and Road Traffic Accident teams were by now handling over 30,000 claims on behalf of the firm's insurer and broker clients every year. Following the opening of Donns 24 hour call centre in March 2002 the firm was appointed by Bennetts (GB) Ltd and Argent Insurance to run their Accident Management Centres. In less than a year the Call Centre had already dealt with 10,000 accidents on behalf of its clients. Colonnade Insurance Brokers also renewed its contract with Donns for a further three years and in 2002 it was anticipated that Donns would handle around 45,000 accident cases on behalf of the insurance broker.

expertise to obtain the very best rehabilitation, and therefore compensation, for their clients. The team recovered over £15 million in damages in 2001 for clients who had suffered serious injuries including spinal and brain injury, amputation and fatalities arising from accidents on the road, at work or in the street.

The Clinical Negligence Department is headed by Stephanie Forman, a lawyer widely recognised as a leading expert in her field. During 2001 Stephanie was instructed to act on behalf of more than 20 Manchester families in connection with organ retention claims against Central Manchester and Manchester Children's University Hospital NHS Trusts. Stephanie has extensive experience with a wide range of complex claims including a number of groundbreaking actions which would contribute to establishing new parameters for compensation payments; she leads a dedicated team which included individuals with combined legal and medical professional qualifications. Areas of particular expertise include still births, orthopaedics, cervical and breast cancer, dental negligence and infant cerebral palsy.

By now the name Donns has also become synonymous with claims for compensation on behalf of armed service veterans suffering from Gulf war Syndrome; the Donns personal injury team has come to be particularly well regarded for its actions against the Ministry of 'Defence. Managing Partner Hilary Meredith is widely regarded as Britain's foremost expert on

A Catastrophic Department had been set up within the overall personal injury range of services and was headed by Managing Partner Hilary Meredith. Hilary and the team of specialised lawyers called upon their particular

Top left: *The Judgment from the landmark American case won by Hilary Meredith on behalf of clients.* **Right:** *Hilary and Raymond receiving Lexcel Accreditation, the Law Society's award for practice management, from the President of the Law Society Michael Napier, 2001.*

Personal Injury claims arising out of military service. In 2001 the department secured the largest pay out ever from the Ministry of Defence, since the changes in the law in 1987 allowed servicemen and women to sue; acting on behalf of a client who sustained extensive injuries whilst serving as a lance corporal in the army Donns were able to obtain an award of £3,670,000.

The department's lawyers have a vast experience in personal injury claims both nationally and internationally and have now firmly

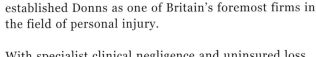

established Donns as one of Britain's foremost firms in the field of personal injury.

With specialist clinical negligence and uninsured loss recovery departments the firm's collective and wide ranging experience in all areas of personal injury contributed to it being appointed to the Legal Aid Board's first Multi Party Action Solicitors Panel.

Meanwhile, in December 2001, Donns would launch its Employers' Liability and Public Claims Liability claims handling department. The newly formed department would represent Donns' continuing commitment to providing a comprehensive range of services within the personal injury field and was expected to deal with some 7,000 cases in its first year.

This Manchester legal eagle has certainly soared above the rest!

Top: *Raymond Donn surrounded by his family, pictured in 1988.*
Far left: *Looking up at The Observatory, Chapel Walk, home to Donns Solicitors.*
Left: *The signing system in the foyer of The Observatory.*

All aboard for the exhibition

When the last train pulled out of Manchester's Central Station in 1969 the future of that unique Victorian building looked bleak indeed; but in fact the future was bright. Whilst the city would be able to cope very well with its two remaining rail terminals to cater for its transport needs the availability of the Central Station site, and its main building, was to provide the opportunity for something that was to become a major boon for communications of a very different kind.

In the middle of the 20th century Manchester had two main exhibition venues. One, now long gone, was at Belle Vue to the east of the city; the other was within 200 yards or so of the present G-MEX site in the building that now houses the Manchester Science Museum.

The demise of those two venues however left Manchester with no significant exhibition hall but, as luck would have it, with the opportunity to create such a facility in the heart of the city. The venue could be easily reached by road and by public transport, the central location would be close to ample hotel accommodation for exhibitors and visitors alike, whilst the many leisure amenities that Manchester can offer would be an attraction in themselves.

Another invaluable advantage that the 26 acre old station site offered was the building itself. Work had begun on the original Central Station as the northern terminus of the Cheshire Lines Committee Railway (later the LMS) in 1875; the finished structure was an almost classical example of the audacity with which our forebears undertook such projects.

Compromise was not a concept widely embraced by Victorian architects, as can be seen in the sweeping ironwork that gave the building its striking frontage. In addition to the huge expanse of cast ironwork and glass that created the roof of the original station building the exterior walls were of traditional brick construction, much of which still remains.

The substructure of the station - platforms, rail beds, booking halls, waiting rooms and the like - cost, at 19th

This page: Two aspects of the G-MEX Centre.

In 1982 proposals for the redevelopment of the Central Station site were first published, having been developed through a unique civic and commercial partnership.

The design brief for local architect Jack Bogle was to blend the best of the old with new construction techniques and materials to create an exhibition and entertainment venue that would cater for the needs of the widest possible spectrum of users. It was also part of the brief that the building should retain its landmark status. To that end, whilst the additional construction that was required to create the main exhibition venue would be striking in its original design, many of the themes of the Victorian building would be retained, and indeed extended into the new areas.

As much as possible of the character and detail of the original was to be kept including 18 massive iron arches supporting the vast single-span roof and the glazing on

century prices £124,000; in addition the roof itself cost some £58,000. By comparison The Manchester International Convention Centre which opened in 2001 would eventually cost £24 million to build.

*Top: A view of G-MEX's vast interior. **Above:** An exhibition taking place in the main exhibition area of the G-MEX Centre. **Right:** The G-MEX Centre at night.*

each gable end. Much of the original blue and pink brickwork would be restored. Often it needed dismantling and rebuilding brick by brick. The station's original iron platform columns were reused to support the all new glazed entrances, bars, restaurants and side walkways. Where ironwork had disintegrated moulds were made to produce completely new castings.

To the casual viewer perhaps the most obvious manifestation of the design brief would be the extensive use of ornamental cast iron that is such a feature of the interior of the building. The 19th century theme also extended to the forecourt and access areas of the building, areas which would be cobbled, very much as they would have been when the station first opened.

Subsequent refurbishment however, mainly in connection with the building of the Manchester International Convention Centre would see the replacement of the cobble frontage with rather more practical forms of paving which, though still very much in keeping with the architectural theme of G-MEX would prove far better for pedestrian use and access for the disabled.

The G-MEX Exhibition Centre was opened by Her majesty the Queen in 1986 and from that moment on rapidly established a reputation as one of the UK's leading exhibition venues, with the facilities that had been designed into the newly opened building proving to be as strong an attraction as the location itself.

The floor space within G-MEX would provide considerable flexibility being able to be divided by special shuttering to create two separate exhibition floors, each complete with its own entrance, foyer, bar and restaurant facilities. This would enable organisers to opt for the space which suited their particular requirements - and for two separate exhibitions to run simultaneously.

The total floor area of the main exhibition halls would be 10,350 square metres, with a height to the roof apex of 26 metres. When divided into two one hall would cover 2,800 square metres and the other 7,500.

Beneath the main building, another legacy of the Victorian structure, is the undercroft, deep brick-lined vaults running the length and depth of the building which could provide car parking for 800 vehicles (the site's total car parking capacity would be 1,500 spaces) on two levels with pedestrian access to ground level via escalators.

Even as work was being completed on the Central Station conversion it was realised that there was also a demand for a facility that could house conferences and seminars of varying sizes - and it was equally obvious that the G-MEX site had the space for further developments along those lines.

The Seminar Centre which opened its doors in 1995 is very much an extension of the main G-MEX structure and, whilst linked directly to it, is also be totally self-contained.

Top right: *A view from the stage into the auditorium of the Seminar Centre.* **Left:** *A Motor Show taking place at the G-MEX Centre.*

There are two levels to the Seminar Centre with the ground floor housing the entrance foyer, Pullman Restaurant, bar and kitchen facilities. On the first floor are the seminar suites, the largest of these providing a floor area of just under 600 square metres having a capacity for 500 delegates. That largest suite is capable of sub-division into three smaller suites of 357,100 and 57 square metres with an additional separate suite on the first floor of 177 square metres.

As the 20th century drew to a close Manchester had several venues designed for conference use, not least the G-MEX Seminar Centre, but there was nothing in the city or its surrounding area that could cater for large-scale conventions.

The creation of the Manchester International Convention Centre coincided with the long awaited redevelopment of the Peter's Field area of the city, of which G-MEX would be a part. The intention was to provide a facility that would be the equal of anything in the UK or Europe in terms of specification, practicality and comfort.

Manchester International Convention Centre (MICC) opened in 2001 to regional and national acclaim. At its heart is a sumptuous theatre style auditorium capable of seating 800 people, and the Great Northern Hall providing some 1,900 square metres of general purpose floor space.

The auditorium features a 250 square metre stage with lift access from ground level, highly sophisticated lighting and sound control systems, and include facilities such as a master control room and booths for simultaneous translation.

The Great Northern Hall also offers complete control of the interior environment and an extensive and uninterrupted floor space making it ideal for small exhibitions. On first floor level, along one side of the hall, would also be seven 'breakout' rooms. The ceiling height throughout the hall would be 10 metres with floor loadings of 3 tonnes per square metre. Kitchen and service facilities would, for the most part, be below ground level.

The innovative design of the MICC both links and integrates it with the Seminar Centre that, in turn, would be connected to the Central and Windsor Exhibition Halls. That configuration has created a self-contained facility in the very centre of Manchester capable of catering for almost every need - even to hosting part of the Commonwealth Games in 2002.

Central Station was a wonder of the Victorian world, today the site it once occupied gives full honours to that noble past whilst simultaneously celebrating the wonders of our new millennium.

Above: *The entrance to the Seminar Centre.*
Below: *Manchester's G-MEX Centre, ready to take a leading role in the Commonwealth Games, 2002.*

Keeping on the road

There are surely few things we dread more these days than to be driving along the motorway and see a red light appear on the dashboard display of our car. Well few worse things other than the even more unwelcome experience of hearing the car engine begin to make the kind of unpleasant noises which tell us that our car, or van, is not going to take us much further. Driving along the road and seeing some poor soul broken down at the side of the road is always an opportunity to thank our lucky stars that it is not us stranded in the wilderness. But if the worst should happen we may be luckier than some. Maybe if we break down we will have the services of a first class recovery service patrolman who can get us back on the road again before we give way to despair and despondency.

On the morning of the 23rd March 1996, a Mr Cooper was driving from Manchester to Stoke on Trent. At 12.30 pm that day his 1600 cc Vauxhall Cavalier broke down. The RAC was called out and the patrolman diagnosed a timing belt failure. A disaster? No. The RAC patrolman contacted the Manchester based firm of GE Sparkes and Co which told the patrolman that its engineers could repair the vehicle in less than two hours. The RAC patrolman towed Mr Cooper's Cavalier to the Sparkes Keele Repair Centre and Mr Cooper was able to drive off at 2pm, not only extremely happy with the service from Sparkes and the RAC but able to carry on with his weekend in Stoke on Trent with very little loss of time - the alternative would have been recovery back to his home in Flixton arriving at 4 pm and a ruined weekend, and still faced with getting his car repaired on the following Monday.

Below: Company founder George Ezra Sparkes with one of his grandchildren.

through the 1960s. Originally George worked on his own but by 1959 he was employing four staff to help in the garage as mechanics and drivers.

Peter Sparkes, George's son, joined the firm in 1970 on the shop floor and worked his way through all aspects of the business. John Boscoe Cummins had started in 1966 as a mechanic and would later become a director and workshop manager.

Today Sparkes recovers or repairs almost 20,000 vehicles each year from our roads, but it had far smaller beginnings.

GE Sparkes & Co. was founded in 1958 by George Ezra Sparkes. George had three brothers all of whom emigrated to Canada whilst George opted to stay at home in Maidstone in Kent.

In his early working life George managed a local farm in Kent but he moved to Manchester in the late 1940s where he took over Chapman's Taxis, based in Chorlton, and which he eventually renamed GE Sparkes & Co. Ltd. At first the firm took on all aspects of motor repairs as well as running taxis and car hire

Justin Sparkes, Peter's son, started in 2001 as breakdown recovery driver and like his father before him would begin working his way through the business.

Sparkes is particularly proud of its ability to retain staff. Long serving employees include John Logan, the recovery manager and Gary Dodd, recovery driver, both of whom began their career with Sparkes in the mid 1980s whilst Russell Davies who started with the company after leaving school in 1978 celebrated 20 years of service in 1998. With such a very high staff

Top: Max, the firm's dog who remained with the company for 15 years and attended all the breakdowns.
Above left: The Chorlton Green premises.

retention rate many have worked for up to 20 years having joined the firm straight from school. Today Sparkes has around 35 employees: mechanics, drivers and office staff dealing with work arriving from individual motorists as well as recovery work from the RAC, Green Flag and other major recovery organisations.

The business occupied Chorlton Green Garage from 1958 until December 2001 when the firm moved to St Modwen Road off Barton Dock Road at Trafford Park.

The new company headquarters would be based on 1.9 acres of land with a central office block and 5,000 sq ft of workshop space enabling the company to offer a full range of services including MOTs, servicing and all mechanical repairs for cars and vans up to 3.5 tonnes.

Geographically the fine site complimented the breakdown recovery operation, being located between a burgeoning industrial zone, and an ever increasing residential area close to the newly developed Trafford Centre. The site, within a quarter of a mile of the M60 Manchester orbital motorway, would allow exceptional access to the whole of Greater Manchester road network allowing for a fast and efficient service. The new premises, open 24 hours a day, also offers a modern waiting room with canteen facilities offering light refreshment for customers as well as allowing customers and patrolmen easy access to the site for the storage or minor repair of vehicles within a safe and secure compound

Top left: The recovery control room. *Above right:* The Secure Compound. *Right:* A line-up of recovery vehicles outside the Chorlton Road premises.

Sadly, George Sparkes died in 1997 and his son Peter Sparkes became the Managing Director alongside John Cummins, who had married George's daughter, and Peter's son, Justin.

Peter had decided in 1980 to go into breakdown recovery at a time when the RAC and AA were beginning to only recover vehicles rather than repair them themselves. Technology, computerisation and new electronics have made engines much more sophisticated - and cars are less frequently repaired at the roadside now and therefore need to be recovered more often.

What was needed was a 24 hour breakdown recovery service with full mechanical repair facilities and with an office and control room open seven days a week. GE Sparkes was happy to oblige.

In 1996 GE Sparkes opened a depot at Stoke on Trent with the same facilities and services as its Manchester depot. Covering the Keele area the new service opened in the Spring of 1996. Although initially based at the Granada services on the M6 motorway in January 1997 the company relocated to a large ex-Renault main agents garage in Wolstanton, Stoke on Trent. The company quickly established itself within the local area continuing the success of its Chorlton operation. Indeed success was demanded by the RAC. When the Keele patch was taken over the rescue-recovery conversion rate was too high (in excess of 25 per cent) and the RAC gave Sparkes a

target to meet of 18 per cent. In the first two years of operating in Keele, GE Sparkes was able to reduce the conversion rate down to a commendable 7.5-10 per cent, thanks to much hard work from both managers and drivers alike. In the Manchester area figures would be even more impressive with recovery-conversion rates of around 3 per cent against a target of 7.5 per cent.

Today the company prides itself on its fleet of vehicles which can cope with all the demands of recovery work. Vehicles are renewed on a regular basis which not only keeps the fleet looking very modern but also ensures that it is able to cope with the changing demands of the industry. The base keeps in touch with its vehicles using mobile phones and turbo despatch systems. By the millennium the firm has no fewer than 22 vehicles all kept to the highest standards, with 5 new vehicles on order and consideration being given to the installation of GPS satellite navigation systems in some vehicles.

With its well earned reputation for fairness and common sense GE Sparkes looks set to continue its remarkable progress for the foreseeable future. In the meantime those of us who frequent the

region's roads in our cars and vans can rest a little easier knowing that if and when that little red light starts its warning winks, our hearts need not sink quite so far as they once might have done. Yes we may still find ourselves on the hard shoulder of the motorway at three o'clock in the morning, but should that unwanted event ever arise at least we can have the comfort and consolation of knowing that there is someone out there who has our interest at heart. Someone who will not only take care of our problem but do so quickly and efficiently. On such dark nights we can perhaps spare a thought for George Ezra Sparkes who back in 1958 started his once tiny company and left a legacy which made travel by car far less hazardous and worrying than it once was.

Top: Drivers line-up in front of their vehicles.
Above left: *Justin Sparkes.* ***Below:*** *Two of the firm's fleet of recovery vehicles.*

Not just any old iron

'Arrghh-an-oone!' When was the last time you heard the unmistakable, if barely comprehensible, cry of a rag and bone man down your road? Did it occur to you then that his once familiar call might be something which would pass into history alongside the Hokey Pokey seller with his ice cream tricycle and the coal man?

Anyone over a certain age can recall with nostalgia the rag and bone man who might give us a goldfish, or a balloon, or a few pence for our old rags and bits of lead piping to take goodness knows where. To small children it was not much of a mystery; we never thought to ask where all that stuff got taken - that was just the way things were. When we got a little older we would realise that our old rags were taken away to be shredded into paper or processed into cloth of some kind - and of course the metal would be sold back to foundries to be melted down and used again.

The rag and bone man with his horse and cart was once part of our everyday world, today's world is very keen on recycling, but that old business was always about recycling old and unwanted goods to turn them into new ones.

One Manchester firm which has made the transition from the horse and cart days to become a huge business with impeccable green credentials is White Reclamation Ltd.

The firm was founded in 1904 when Harry Wood, the grandfather of the present chairman Stewart White, began working as a rag and bone man. Though perhaps rag and bone 'man' is something of a misnomer since Harry, who had been brought up in an orphanage, was just 14 years old when he began his working life. Still it was a job, and if it was not a very glamorous one at least it required few qualifications and would provide a living for a hard working young man, perhaps not a fortune but quite enough to marry on and to raise a family.

Between the wars Harry Wood's rag and bone business evolved into dealing in scrap metal, though the firm would never operate as a traditional scrap yard dealing in wrecked cars and the like. The economic boom which followed the end of the Great War in 1918 had proved to be short-lived and after 1929 the hungry thirties gave an unexpected boost to what we would now call recycling - though mass unemployment and the ease with which anyone could take up the rag and bone business made for fierce competition and hard times for everyone, not least Harry Wood and his family. With an eye on the future the founder eventually took his son into the firm to work with him. Sadly Harry Wood's son, also Harry, worked in the business for only a few years before dying in 1946 at the early age of only 33.

Below: *Harry Wood with his one horse-powered transportation, in the early 1900s.*

The company was then developed by Stewart to become a supplier of steel furnace feed to home-based steel works and to foundries specialising in new production steel from scrap.

Major contracts in those years were to take away scrap from the Royal Ordnance factory, Gardner Engines and Redpath Dorman Long plus a selection of steel profile cutters throughout Lancashire. The scrap was then processed and sold to firms such as British Steel, Baxi Heating and Horwich Castings.

In 1983 the company moved to an eight acre site on the A57, the company's present site on Liverpool Road, Peel Green, Eccles. The move would make considerable expansion possible.

The business became a limited company in 1958 as H Wood (Patricroft) Ltd. At that time the company traded from a half acre site adjacent to the Bridgewater Canal in Patricroft. Due to Harry Wood's age however and the lack of help the company had little success and when Harry's grandson Stewart White took charge in 1961 the firm was heavily in debt.

Stewart ran the company for his grandfather for the next five years. When the founder died in 1966 the company's debts combined with death duties took Stewart the rest of the decade to pay off.

Top: *Some of the firm's vehicles in the early 1970s.*
Above left and right: *Sorting recyclable material on the yard in the 1970s.*

Stewart White's eldest son, Steve, joined the company from college in 1984 soon after the move to Peel Green. In the mid 1980s, in a prelude of things to come, a small waste division was developed, mainly handling waste foundry sand.

By 1990 company turnover was £6 million, but no more expansion in processing scrap metal could be achieved in the UK due to the demise of heavy

of the environment had, in fact, being going on for many years perhaps beginning with the clean air legislation of the 1950s following the deaths of thousands of Londoners in pea souper fogs. Clean Air Acts had led gradually to the demise of coal fires and the coalman; now environmental consciousness was beginning to pervade everywhere with ever more demands for legislation to prevent pollution and improper dumping of waste materials.

Alongside those demands for a better environment was an increasing fear that natural resources would run out if the world did not husband nature's bounty. Fears that raw materials might eventually run out had been given international publicity by the Club of Rome in the late 1960s, which had even predicted that oil would run out by the 1990s. Despite that false prophecy, two decades later demand for recycling of wood, plastics and metals were louder than ever. If ever there was a good time for a

industry. In addition foundry business looked to be disappearing; limited scrap supplies and the potentially decreasing markets made the company look to its increasing knowledge of the waste disposal industry whilst new planning and licensing regulations provided the impetus for a conscious decision to switch the firm's focus to recycling.

The green movement had been gaining ground for some years already. Green party candidates had not been too successful in gaining seats in government but they had received many thousands of votes testifying to increasing concern about the environment, fears which had been given additional impetus during the 1960s and were by now beginning to bear ever increasing fruit. The clean up

This page: *The yard and the company's fleet of vehicles in the 1990s.*

to improve recycling percentages, with an aim to one day achieving 100 per cent recovery and recycling.

Not that this is the only aim of the business. New opportunities are continually being looked at by the White family - within the group there is also a Closed Circuit Television and Security systems business Mono Alarm Installations Ltd.

Despite many changes the company remains a family one: David White, Stewart's second son, has been with the company since 1998 after a career playing professional football for Manchester City, Leeds United, Sheffield United and England.

Today Stewart is Chairman, Steve White is Managing Director and David, too, is a Director alongside Commercial Director, Mark Hutchinson.

company to begin moving into waste disposal and recycling this was surely it.

The first major waste disposal contract for White Reclamation was with Manpower Services to clear the area under what is now the G Mex site.

Major new clients would be MEL Chemicals, Proctor and Gamble, and PPG Industries in addition to Horwich Castings.

In the process of transforming itself into a new kind of business H Wood (Patricroft) Ltd changed its name to White Reclamation Ltd and took on board new staff with a more intimate knowledge of waste management.

The change proved a wise one. Due to landfill tax regulations and to waste regulations recycling, not simply dumping or burying waste, would become ever more important.

Today the reputation of White Reclamation rests on its quality of service and its high recycling percentages. And multi million pound plant on the company's site continues

'Where there's muck there's brass' may have been a philosophy which satisfied our Victorian forefathers but it is not a view which will find much support today. Thanks to firms like White Reclamation the world is a cleaner, safer place. Furthermore we can share a sense of pride that the world's resources are being used more wisely than they have in the past as we actively embrace the thrifty ways of our forbears and like them recycle our old things - even if today, sadly, the people that do it for us no longer drive down our streets with a horse and cart shouting 'Arrghh-an-oone!'

Top left: *The company viewed from a distance.* ***Above left:*** *One of the new recycling vehicles leaving the company, 2001.* ***Right:*** *Group Chairman, Stewart White (left) and Managing Director, Steven White.*

Home improvements

I t's funny how the world of kitchens, bedrooms and bathrooms has changed over the years.

Those whose memories stretch back far enough in time will recall the days before fitted everything was the order of the day. Those whose memories stretch back before the 1950s will recall Manchester life which seems, to the younger generation, so distant it might as well be another planet. Go back some decades, but still well within living memory, and we had no televisions to watch let alone automatic washing machines. Mother doing the washing on Monday might have involved a washing machine, but as often as not washday meant the tub and posser or the scrubbing brush and washboard. Cooking was perhaps more familiar, there cannot have been many folk left who still cooked over an open fire, but the gas and electric cookers of the 1950s were still a long way from the micro-waves and split level integrated cookers with fitted extractor fans that we take as normal today.

The idea of consumer goods was pretty alien to a generation brought up between the wars who, in the bad days of the 1930s were more worried about where the rent money was coming from than buying a new wireless, let alone what today we call a hi-fi unit. But by the end of the 1950s after a generation long slump people began to have money in their pockets once again. By the 1960s demand was even greater and by the 1970s demand for new and better white goods - the trade term for cookers, fridges and washing machines - was still increasing as what had

seemed luxuries to an earlier generation were now seen as the basic necessities of life.

Many new retail outlets sprang up to meet this ever-increasing demand. Many old retail firms fell by the wayside unable to change to meet new customer needs; many of the new firms were short lived, unable to grasp the need to not only sell goods but to provide a service which ensured that customers would return again and again. One new firm which did not ignore that basic business principle was Manchester's own A&S Domestic Services.

Established in 1977 by husband and wife team Alan and Sue Forrest, A&S Domestic Services is without doubt one of the region's, indeed England's, leading suppliers of household appliances.

With unfaltering commitment and determination Alan and Sue would achieve a level of success even they could not have imagined those long years ago.

With eight premises on Barlow Moor Road, Chorlton by the mid 1990s the company had already supplemented its home appliance sales with spares and repairs and reconditioned appliances (refurbished in the company's own

Top right: *Sue Forrest with some of the staff at A&S circa 1992.* ***Left:*** *Company founders Alan and Sue Forrest, outside one of their shops.*

purpose built workshop).

Over the years the company had built up excellent links with many of the world's leading appliance manufacturers enabling it to offer unrivalled levels of value and expertise.

By the late 90s customers visiting the recently built, air conditioned showroom would find more than 400 products on display. From washing machines to vacuum cleaners, fridge-freezers to dishwashers, a massive selection was to be found. And of course there were prices to suit every budget, with all the latest models on offer.

Importantly, those having trouble finding exactly what they wanted found that members of the ever-helpful sales team remained as happy as ever to discuss their needs with them.

Attention to customer care has been the backbone of the company's success throughout.

Top: Some of the firm's delivery vehicles.
Above left: Sue Forrest inside one of the company's stores. Right: Advertising hoardings in the prestigious Trafford Centre.

People return time and time again to A&S because they know they will always receive good value and a quality service.

In addition to its retail business A&S also provides a first rate spares service to the trade. And there too Alan and Sue are committed to putting the customer first. To Alan and Sue all customers are special, without them they could never have achieved the success they have done.

A&S is the epitome of the family run business. As well as Alan and Sue, by the 1990s son John would be working for them as a Service Engineer whilst daughter Adele Lock commenced her impressive career employed in the accounts department alongside her cousin Kelly. Son-in-law Matthew Lock would

take responsibility for the all important purchasing role and daughter-in-law, Lisa Forrest would also find an opening in Accounts. Alan's son, Alan Forrest Jnr. completes the picture having been appointed Spares Manager in 1999.

It was Adele's appointment that proved a pivotal moment in creating the A&S of today. Rapidly progressing to the position of General Manager, her flare and dynamism added fresh impetus to the company. Her early contributions to the development of marketing and administration processes proved to be invaluable setting a solid foundation for further growth.

And so it was that in April 2000, from modest early beginnings (trading in recondi- tioned domestic appliances) and still guided by Alan and Sue's vision and commercial acumen, the company 'went limited' having by that time enjoyed several years of enviable growth; annual turnover of seven figures a milestone long ago passed. By this time the firm employed 35 people working variously within Sales, Engineering, Distribution, Adminis- tration, Marketing and IT. Reconditioned goods had long time ago lost ground to brand new and the range of

services had evolved by logical increments to now include home interiors, building services and computers.

By Spring 2002, the firm had re-branded itself. A&S Domestic Services based at 257-259 Barlow Moor Road, Chorlton since 1990 had developed beyond all recognition. Now as The A&S Group, long established as one of the leading outlets for home appliances in the North West, the company had firmly positioned itself as one of Greater Manchester's leading suppliers of fitted kitchens, bedrooms and bathrooms and with many home improve- ments involving building work, the creation of A&S Building Services proved to be a further inspirational step.

With such a diverse range of services and operations and yet retaining a modestly sized workforce, the company clearly had needed to develop along a sound business model. Simply

Top: An A&S delivery vehicle in Coronation Street.
Inset*: Glowing testimony from actor John Savident (Fred Elliott) who obviously feels he received a square deal from A&S.* ***Above****: Johnny Briggs (the Street's Mike Baldwin) obviously shares the same views on A&S as Fred.*

stated, the A&S formula would be about attracting talented and adaptable people and supporting them with the best systems and technology possible. In pursuit of that aim the company created three strategic roles, Human Resources Manager, IT Manager and Accounts Manager; incumbents to each role having specific aims and objectives that would embrace recruitment, training, systems development and finance; enabling the company, whenever it found itself considering a further business venture, to do so in the knowledge that it would have the right people and the right systems in place with all elements being under tight financial control.

The foundations for such a strategy had been laid long ago through a brilliant piece of forward thinking by Alan Forrest Snr. Even in the late 80s when computers were in their relative infancy, Alan foresaw the potential of this burgeoning technology. Following introduction to a talented young computer programmer named Gareth Connor, Alan had been left so impressed that he proposed a partnership between the two. The result was a software development company, initially called Suresoft (later to become Adaptev), that specialised in the design of bespoke business solutions. Through this alliance, Alan was able to bring great advantages to bear upon A&S Domestic Services. Based adjacent to the A&S site, the two organisations would enjoy a close and symbiotic relationship. With Adaptev using A&S both as a model and test bed for the development and refinement of its products, A&S would inevitably be the first to enjoy the fruits of the software designers labours, obtaining leading edge technology and support at minimal costs. As a result, A&S refined its management and accounting practices immeasurably using Adaptev's know-how and through adoption of one of their most innovative developments A&S would, by Summer 2002, operate a fully integrated sales, services, stock, purchasing and accounting system via one extremely powerful and dynamic business computing framework.

By the opening years of the 21st century A&S Domestic Services has built up an unequalled reputation for supplying and servicing quality domestic appliances at excellent prices and most importantly providing a superior after sales service.

In addition, having opened a new 12,500sq.ft. warehouse in Salford in 2001, providing more space and more stock under one roof, greater purchasing opportunities presented themselves that were quickly exploited enabling the home appliance side of the business to remain buoyant in an increasingly competitive market dominated by the major chains.

Despite its remarkable growth since its foundation the company still remains a family run business, now employing over 40 staff at its site in Barlow Moor Road, Chorlton. The business continues to steadily extend its client base beyond its traditional Greater Manchester boundaries and nation-wide deliveries have become an increasingly regular feature of life for the firm's fleet of delivery vehicles. Technology has further widened its business horizons significantly with on-line orders having been received form places as far apart as the Falkland Islands, Kuwait and Australia.

No account of A&S would be complete without mention of the invaluable contribution over the years to be made by John Higgins. In a story full of achievement and continual change (not without its peaks and troughs) John has remained a constant throughout. In later years retained as a financial consultant, he was the Company's original and longest serving accountant. He will always be considered a true friend of the business and family.

By the time of the company's 25th anniversary in 2002 the original A&S - Alan and Sue Forrest - could look back with a well earned sense of pride at their joint venture tentatively begun back in 1977, a business that has grown to become an impressive testimonial to their hard work and commitment.

Top left: *Another successful advertisement.*
Below: *Sue and Alan Forrest.*

The Athens of the North

According to the Victorian Prime Minster Benjamin Disraeli 'If rightly understood Manchester was as great a human exploit as Athens'. Disraeli could have been making favourable comparison between the intellectual opportunities in Manchester and those offered by the long-famed philosophers of classical Greece.

And those opportunities are even greater now than they were in Disraeli's time. Today's UMIST, with its many thousands of students, is ranked as one of the UK's great centres of study and research; it has won three Queen's Awards for Higher Education and two Queen's Awards for Export Achievement and is one of the most highly decorated universities in the UK. UMIST is still at the heart of Manchester, just as it was intended to be more than 175 years ago.

The story of UMIST has its roots in the early 19th century when several local men met in the Bridgewater Arms in High Street to establish a Mechanics' Institute in Manchester where artisans could be taught, by part-time study, the basic principles of mechanics and chemistry. Of the hundreds of such institutions founded around that time Manchester's alone has thrived.

That famous meeting was convened on 7th April 1824 by G Wood. In the chair was Sir Benjamin Heywood a prosperous banker; others who attended were: Robert Hyde Greg, a cotton mill owner and soon-to-be MP; Peter Ewart, millwright and engineer; Richard Roberts, machine tools inventor; David Bellhouse, a builder and William Henry who pioneered scientific chemical industry and developed his business into fizzy drinks. William Fairburn, the versatile engineer whose name is associated with water wheels and machinery of every kind and the Britannia tubular bridge but above all with scientific engineering, was elected first Secretary; he was later knighted. Also present was John Dalton who became father of Atomic Theory and who would become the Vice President in 1840. Sir Benjamin Heywood would be President for the first 17 years.

Thus the Manchester Mechanics' Institution was established in 1824, entirely through private initiative and funds. The Institute's first purpose built building would be

Top left: A policeman stands to attention outside the University's main entrance in 1902. ***Below:*** *The practical nature of the university's courses are illustrated in this 1902 photograph of the plumbers laboratory. **Below left:** Alcock and Brown, the first men to fly across the Atlantic. Arthur Whitton Brown had attended the Manchester Municipal College of Technology in the early 1900s.*

A period of planning, reorganisation and discussion between the city, the Technical School and the University of Manchester ensued, with fact-finding deputations going to the Continent and to the USA.

in Cooper Street and was opened in 1827, followed in 1856 by a new building on Princess Street. In 1883 John Henry Reynolds, Secretary of the Mechanics' Institute since 1879, reorganised the Institute as a technical school using the schemes and examinations of the City and Guilds' of London Institute. The Technical Instruction Act of 1889, which owed much to the influence of Manchester men, led to taxation providing general financial support for technical education for the first time. The Technical School also benefited much, in terms of land and other resources, through the legacy of Sir Joseph Whitworth and the Royal Jubilee exhibition held in Trafford Park in 1887.

A transfer from the Whitworth Trust to the Manchester Corporation occurred in 1892 and the Institute was restyled the Municipal Technical School with instruction provided on four sites.

*Top left: The main university building pictured prior to the second world war. **Top right:** Sir John Cockroft, UMIST graduate and Nobel Prize winner for Physics. **Above left:** Roy Chadwick, UMIST graduate, designer of the Lancaster and other aeroplanes. **Right:** An aerial view of Manchester from the 1950s; the university can be seen in the centre of the picture.*

The building which now forms the western end of the present main building in Sackville Street was begun in 1895 and was opened by Prime Minister Arthur Balfour in October 1902.

Already the 'Tech' had pioneered Chemical Engineering as an academic subject in Britain, as it was to do immediately after the first world war with Management Studies. But the major leap forward was the setting up within that burgeoning college of a then relatively small Faculty of Technology of the University of Manchester for work to degree standard leading to BSc Tech and MSc Tech qualifications; this was established in 1905 and was to be the forerunner of the modern UMIST.

There was a further renaming of the institution as the Manchester Municipal College of Technology in 1918 - and celebration the following year when Arthur Whitten

Brown, a graduate of the college, gained international fame as one half of Alcock and Brown, the daring aviators who became the first men to fly across the Atlantic Ocean.

The period between the two world wars was marked by the Depression and the decline of the Lancashire cotton industry in the 1920s and 1930s. This was a time of consolidation and maintaining links with the City, and one in which part-time courses were of major importance to the region. Full implementation of plans for an extension to the new building, needed almost immediately after the 1902 opening, was now delayed - in fact until 1957. Nevertheless ONC, HND and PhD qualifications were introduced and research was revitalised, starting in the 1921-23 period. By 1949 over 8,500 students were recruited.

Dr BV Bowden (later Lord Bowden of Chesterfield) became Principal in 1953 and the great period of expansion of the campus and of disciplines began. In 1955-56 the Manchester College of Science and Technology, as it had become, achieved independent university status under its Royal Charter and separate funding from the University Grants Committee.

In 1966 all non-degree work was moved to the Manchester Polytechnic, now Manchester Metropolitan University, and that same year the College of Science and Technology now became UMIST - the University of Manchester Institute of Science and Technology. Professor Harold Hankins was

Top left: *George Sanders, Hollywood Movie Star and UMIST graduate.* ***Above right:*** *Prime Minister Harold Wilson, during a visit to UMIST in the 1960s (Wilson's father was a UMIST graduate).* ***Right:*** *The unchanging main entrance to the university pictured in the 1980s.*

appointed Principal in 1984, and became UMIST's first Principal and Vice-Chancellor in 1994.

It was in the last quarter of the 20th century that UMIST's story of growth and development into a major international research based university would take place. In the last decade of the second millennium UMIST would not only win Queen's Prizes for Higher Education and Export but also two Prince of Wales' Awards for Innovation and the DTI Award for Technology Transfer. UMIST would perform well in the UK's Research Assessment Exercise in 2002 with all its departments rated 4, 5 or 5*.

Yet the story is not one simply of pure academia; throughout its history UMIST has had close links with industry. In 1968 UMIST established the first industry/academia liaison group - now called UMIST Ventures - which supervises technology transfer and research contracts which lead to successful spin-off companies in hi-tech areas. UMIST's specialities include Paper Science,

Textiles and Language Engineering amongst the more specialist areas, as well as highly rated leading edge Departments and Centres such as Biomolecular Sciences, Corrosion and Protection, the Management School and Atmospheric Physics.

The Satake Centre for Grain Process Engineering is another example of UMIST leading the field. With a donation of £815,000 from the Satake Corporation of Japan, UMIST has taken a world lead in grain processing research, looking at milling, brewing, baking, and processing. A Centre for Microporous Materials has been established with a consortium of industrial companies, whilst UMIST teams have been actively involved in the North Sea oil fields where the university's mechanical engineers have been developing explosive underwater demolition techniques for dismantling oil platforms, whilst other chemistry research teams have produced a unique organophosphate-based retardant that increases the setting time of cement for use by the drilling industry.

Even more remarkably UMIST optometry researchers have helped the blind to see, developing computer software that turns shape and movement into sound - programs inspired by a mnemonic system used by Australian Aborigines to map their world in songs - for instance ascending notes would mean an uphill route.

Elsewhere the Federal School of Business and Management, created in 1994, combined the forces of UMIST's Manchester School of Management with Manchester University's three management and research centres to provide 'cradle to grave' management education from undergraduate degrees to post-graduate training and executive programmes.

Of UMIST's multi million pound budget only some 40 per cent comes from government funding yet the staff and students who take part in over 200 separate courses remain at the forefront of industrially relevant projects. Meanwhile UMIST honours its past as much as its present; it was the founder of what is now the Greater Manchester Museum of Science and Industry, where alumni such as Nobel Laureate, Sir John Cockcroft and aviation pioneer Sir Arthur Whitten Brown, amongst many others, are duly honoured.

From small beginnings UMIST is now a major international research university. Those early industrialists who founded their mechanics' institute so long ago might not have understood genetic engineering or computational fluid dynamics but they would have understood the ethos of today's UMIST which remains true to their intentions.

Top: UMIST in the 1990s.
Above left: *Biological Time-of-Flight Secondary Ion Mass Spectroscopy.* **Right:** *Terry Leahy, Tesco's Chief Executive and the new Chancellor of UMIST.*

Accounting for the years

I n 1885 Queen Victoria had already been on the throne for nearly fifty years. The British Empire coloured a large portion of the map of the world pink, and Britain dominated world trade, as it's Industrial Revolution continued to thrive. In 1885 the British Prime Minister, Gladstone, was advocating home rule for Ireland and the average British worker measured his daily wage in pennies, not pounds. And in that year two accountants, George Poppleton and Charles Appleby, met in Birmingham and decided to go into business together.

The original office was in Lionel Street, Birmingham and from the very beginning they specialised in insolvency cases. Although at the time British industry was booming, the attraction of high profits encouraged factory owners to expand too quickly. Poppleton & Appleby prospered with their specialised knowledge of insolvency and of the engineering trade. Expansion followed and offices were opened in several other cities in the country where heavy industry was flourishing; soon everyone knew 'P & A'.

A Manchester office was eventually opened in Lloyd Street and run by Harry Shipton and Reg Brocklebank: they rapidly became known as two likeable and shrewd 'characters' of the Manchester business scene. Sadly Reg Brocklebank died in 1961, whilst still in his prime, but Harry Shipton carried on for another ten years before retiring.

Arthur Wainwright, who had joined the firm in 1959, then took over the leadership; over the next few years the firm grew considerably. Arthur was ably supported by Peter Lomas, who had joined the firm in 1961, and who later became a partner. Denis Kilroy joined in 1971 and he too became a partner. During the next two decades hardly a meeting of creditors was held in the city without 'P & A' being present and Keith Chadwick became well known for asking the awkward questions - though always in a gentlemanly manner.

Originally the cases dealt with were mainly those involving the manufacturing industries but as Manchester has continually changed over the years so the range of cases has widened. The 1960s brought a whole rush of failed restaurants and night-clubs. Many a pop group and cabaret artist who went on to achieve international fame appeared at clubs being supervised by 'P & A', whilst a new owner was sought. As manufacturing has given way to service industries, and 1986 brought a new Insolvency Act, 'P & A' has continued to take on board the challenges of an ever-changing business world. Cases now handled cover the whole range of insolvency, from the individual with bank guarantee problems through to public companies with cash flow difficulties.

Below: *A photograph taken in the garden of George Poppleton's home, in 1910, at a Garden Party given to celebrate 25 years of Poppleton and Appleby. George is seated in the middle of the front row.*

and Stephen Lord, who have already clocked up over twenty years service each, and have already been partners for several years, carrying on.

Over the years 'P &A' has received many offers to become part of the big accountancy empires, a compliment to its expertise and reputation as honest brokers. So far the firm has politely turned down such offers, remaining fiercely loyal to its existing client base and to its long serving staff.

By the time of Queen's Golden Jubilee in 2002, when Elizabeth II had been on the throne for fifty years the British Empire was a thing of the past and Britain no longer dominated world trade and on occasions its economy suffered from events elsewhere. In sport certain footballers earned more in a year than the average man does in a lifetime. And

After a few years at Royal Buildings, Mosley Street the firm moved on and since 1977 'P & A' has been based at 32 High Street, being fortunate enough to survive the Manchester bomb in 1996 when so many nearby buildings were badly damaged. By the opening years of the new century Arthur Wainwright, Denis Kilroy and Keith Chadwick have retired and Peter Lomas will soon join them after having spent forty-one years with the firm. The future of the firm is secure however with Stephen Wainwright

in politics British Prime Minister Blair was still wrestling with problems in Ireland.

Though much may have changed in other spheres, in the world of accountancy the successors to George Poppleton & Charles Appleby the 'P&A' firm of accountants is still going strong.

*Top left: 31 Lloyd Street, the first Manchester office. **Left:** Arthur Wainwright. **Top right:** Denis Kilroy. **Right:** Peter Lomas.*

Audacity and wisdom

It is not every school that can claim a history stretching back almost 500 years. Manchester Grammar School however is a member of an exclusive club whose story reaches back to the 16th century.

It was in 1516 that the Bishop of Exeter, Hugh Oldham, a Lancastrian by birth, paid five pounds to buy a piece of land near the River Irk on which to build a school. By August 1518 when the school opened its doors at Long Millgate the total cost of building had come to 218 pounds 13 shillings and fivepence.

Not content however with simply paying for the building Hugh Oldham also endowed the school with land by the river, and the profits from water driven corn mills. Making the school legally Lord of the Manor, with the power to require its tenants to use its mills, ensured future income. The school's first master was William Plessington who was paid £10 a year.

Boys could be admitted to the school from any part of the country provided they suffered from no contagious disease such as 'pox, leprosy, or pestilence'. The school rules were strict, reflecting the concerns of the times: boys were not allowed to carry knives or staves, nor to indulge in cock fighting or jousting. Astonishing to the present generation of pupils, lessons at the new school began at six in the morning in summer and seven in the winter!

By 1770 the number of boys had increased from 100 to around 150. An additional building had been brought into use in 1776 but by 1808 the growth of Manchester had led to an unhappy change in the school's environs. The site had become surrounded by old buildings chiefly occupied by 'poor people in situations neither healthy nor comfortable'. Additionally Long Millgate was the venue for the thrice weekly Apple Market.

The road was frequently crowded with horses and carts making it difficult for pupils to make their way from the school to the masters' houses where they boarded. Temptation abounded with older boys resorting to the local taverns and consorting with unsuitable women.

Long Millgate stank from the River Irk which had become an open sewer. The boys were expected to play in the street in front of taverns, warehouses and second rate undertakers. It would unfortunately take many years to resolve the school's accommodation problems.

The appointment of Frederick William Walker known as 'Malleus philosophorum' - the hammer of the philosophers - as High Master in 1859 with his stern emphasis on academic attainment led initially to a falling off of pupil numbers.

Word however eventually got around that despite its insalubrious surroundings, uncompromising academic excellence could be found at Manchester Grammar School.

By 1873 the school had 500 pupils and just three years later 750.

In 1868 the school had bought more land in Long Millgate for £1,000 and in 1871 took

*Top centre: Long Millgate pictured in the late 1800s. The 1880 Grammar School building can be seen at the end of the street. **Top right:** Alderley Park Camp, 1904. **Right:** The gymnasium pictured in the early 1900s.*

English Centre; two language laboratories; an indoor swimming pool; a gymnasium; squash courts; separate junior and senior libraries; a theatre and lecture theatre; a careers room, a bookshop, run by the pupils themselves, two computer laboratories; 19 science laboratories; new Art Halls; CDT workshops; Music School; 6th Form Common Rooms and a new Sports Hall.

Around 210 new pupils from 550 applicants are admitted to the student roll each year. Pupils are drawn from every kind of background, many taking advantage of the numerous bursaries available to help towards the cost of attending this foremost independent school. An egalitarian approach given even greater emphasis by the establishment at the start of the new millennium of a multi-million pound fund made possible by generous gifts and pledges. The School's results at A Level and GCSE are consistently among the very best in the country with upwards of 200 boys a year going on into Higher Education and anywhere between 40 and 60 boys a year gaining entry to Oxford or Cambridge.

As the school approaches its five hundredth birthday it can look forward to its second half millennium with confidence that it will continue to live up to its motto Sapere Aude daring its pupils to be wise.

over a new building which had cost £28,000. By October 1880 a gymnasium costing £40,000 had also been added to the school's property. Further building in 1913 transformed narrow Long Millgate into a spacious quadrangle.

It was not enough: in September 1931 at a cost of £240,000 the whole school moved to a new site at Fallowfield, a brick subdued neo-Georgian building. A new and incredibly short school day, 9.30 am to 3.45 pm, was instituted to accommodate day boys travelling from far and wide. Today the Fallowfield site bears witness to many more improvements with £4.5 million spent on new buildings in the 1990s. The new buildings include a new

Top left: *The Queen on her visit to the school in 1965.*
Above left: *Morning assembly in the Memorial Hall.*
Right: *Prince Charles pictured during his visit to the school in 1999.* ***Below:*** *The School pictured from the extensive playing fields.*

Girl power

Withington Girls' School was founded in 1890 by a group of Mancunians including Mr CP Scott, the first editor of the Manchester Guardian, and Mr Henry Simon of Simon Engineering fame, along with his wife Emily. The foresight and generosity of the latter would provide the school's extensive grounds and playing fields.

Together with Miss Caroline Herford, Mrs Louise Lejeune and Dr Adolphus Ward these visionary men and women determined to establish a school that would provide the same educational opportunities for their daughters as were then available for their sons.

Withington Girls' School opened at 16 Mauldeth Road. A house committee was formed to obtain estimates for painting, wallpapering and other necessary repairs. There were several early problems: the landlord was asked to repair the leaking roof and Bailey (whose firm did the plumbing for the school for over 70 years) was asked on no fewer than three occasions to investigate the unpleasant smell in a bedroom! But some problems were never resolved: the fires smoked and the drains were seriously defective.

Top centre: *A very early picture of Withington Girls' School, circa 1910.* **Right:** *Miss Stansfield (2nd right) Principal of Bedford Physical Training College, when she opened the new gym in June 1934.* **Below:** *The whole school pictured in autumn 2001.*

Despite these domestic difficulties the school thrived; growing numbers meant that by 1903 larger premises were needed. The new building was then on the edge of farmland and Wellington Road was no more than a cart track. 'Woodlands', the core of the current building, had been built in 1888 by Mr L Pughe as an independent boys' school; it was bought for £3,000 and Mr Pughe moved his boys to North Wales.

In 1905 an outbreak of sore throats led not only to the school being closed for three weeks, but also to the first of the 'new' buildings. Mrs Simon offered to buy a small Cottage Sanatorium which was erected on the north-west corner of the site. It remained there for over 30 years before being moved nearer to the school to

become the Staff Room. Though seldom used for infectious ailments the building proved extremely useful for cricket and hockey teas and for Saturday morning cookery classes. The next major extension, built in 1913, cost £225 7s 11d and now looks like part of the original building .

The school has continued to develop and expand throughout its history. Electricity was installed in 1923, removing the anxiety before entertainments lest something should happen to the gas lighting in the gymnasium.

The provision of a new gymnasium with an expensive pyengadu (Burmese ironwood) floor, followed by a state of the art chemistry laboratory in 1934, reflected the continuing commitment to the founders' vision of a school where physical and scientific education, rarely offered with rigour to girls, formed part of a broad curriculum. That commitment remains just as strong today as it did throughout the 20th century.

From 1908 until the end of the century four long-serving headmistresses ensured that Withington's development kept pace with the times. Miss MA Grant (1908-1938), Miss ME Bain (1938-1961), Miss M Hulme (1961-1985) and Mrs M Kenyon (1986-2000) all brought imagination and vision to their plans for the school. Under them the school prospered and its academic standards never wavered. At the start of the new millennium under the leadership of its Headmistress, Mrs JD Pickering, Withington Girls' School would continue to be consistently ranked amongst the top ten girls' schools in the country. And the school continues to excel in its extra-curricular provision as well as academic results. The school values its links with the local Manchester community - many older pupils enjoying their experience of voluntary work with the elderly or the young in neighbouring schools and hospitals. WGS girls would also be committed to raising funds for charities close to home and further afield: the school having close links with two schools and a hospital in Kenya and contributing to several projects to improve the lives of its African friends. At the start of a new century Withington's staff and pupils would rejoice in being part of the multi-cultural city of Manchester with its universities, concert halls, theatres and sports facilities. And, despite its Victorian origins, the school is a friendly, warm community providing a wealth of opportunity for the young woman of the 21st century. Undoubtedly the founders would be proud of their legacy.

*Top left: The Chemistry Laboratory. **Above left:** Trampolining in the new Sports Hall. **Right:** An aerial view of Withington Girls' School in 2001.*

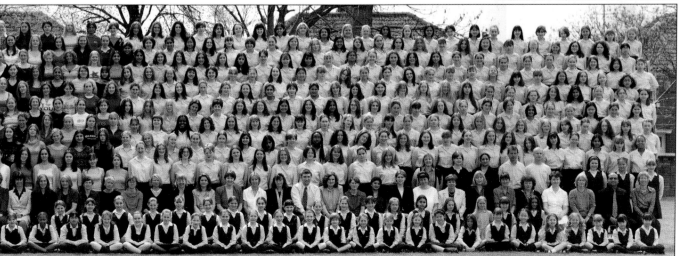

Salford's shining centre

Colgate toothpaste and Palmolive soap are amongst the most readily recognised product brands in the world. And the name of Colgate-Palmolive Ltd has been associated with Salford since 1938.

The Colgate-Palmolive story began in 1806 when 23 year old William Colgate opened a soap and candle factory in New York. Some 84 years later Caleb Johnson, the son of the founder of Johnson Soap, developed the famous Palmolive soap made from olive and palm oils. By 1917 the brand was so famous Johnson's changed its name to the Palmolive company.

In 1926 Palmolive merged with a firm founded in 1872 by the Peet brothers to form the Palmolive-Peet company. Two years later that new company merged with Colgate to become Colgate-Palmolive-Peet. Not until 1953 would the name become simply Colgate-Palmolive.

The British end of the business began in 1913 when the first tablets of Palmolive soap were imported. A UK subsidiary was formed in 1922 and premises were acquired for the production of toothpaste and other toiletries, though soap was still being imported.

In 1938 however a soap production plant was acquired in Ordsall Lane, Salford. The site would eventually become one of the largest plants of its kind in Europe.

Built in 1870 the Ivy Soap Works, in Ordsall Lane, were bought from Charles W Goodwin. Until the 1990s the name Goodwin Soap Works could still be seen on the old building that had been used to house the Colgate-Palmolive Medical Centre, Cash sales and the Social Club.

*Left: Staff pictured inside the factory circa 1958. **Below:** The Colgate-Palmolive factory pictured in 1942.*

which would last until 1985.

More expansion followed in 1976 when the Spillers-French site was acquired and the buildings demolished - with the exception of the Lucas warehouse which became part of the site warehouse system and at one time housed the export department, the rest of the site becoming a company car park.

In the following two years Colgate Palmolive bought the Boxmakers works and the Corporation land

During the first two years of the second world war a new kettle house and soap finishing building were erected along with a new boiler house. The new kettle house held ten soap kettles each 15ft 6in in diameter with a capacity of 4,370 cubic feet. The new building provided the site with 48,000 sq ft of production area.

The company's toothpaste operation was transferred to Salford from London in 1950. Seven years later the company's Research and Development Department also came to Salford.

Another building programme, completed in 1949, had added a further 108,000 sq ft to the main building to provide what was then the Toilet Articles Department. In the mid 1950s a further 137,000 sq ft were added to this building.

'Liquids' production was started in 1962 when a five storey extension to the building on what was by now called the Springfield site was completed adding yet another 190,000 sq ft.

A fire at an adjacent site belonging to RW Paul which destroyed its premises in 1965 allowed Colgate-Palmolive to acquire an additional 1.3 acres, though it was not until 1972 that the St George's and Springfield buildings were acquired and nappy or 'diaper' production could begin, production

alongside and up to the Martindale Street boundary; the company also purchased the Co-op Tea warehouse which occupied another 1.3 acres of land.

Colgate Palmolive's final land acquisition in Salford took place in 1980 when it bought the Bloomer Holt Timber Yard obtaining another 5.9 acres.

At the end of the 1980s the old Medical Centre, Cash sales and Social Club were demolished to make way for what would become the company car park near its number one lodge. All the departments involved, apart from the Social Club, were rehoused in the main factory. At the same time the Spillers-French site along with the St George's, Boxmakers and the Corporation land were leased to the St Modwen company for development. The former RW Paul site along with the Co-op Tea warehouse site and the lease for the Bloomer Holt site were sold for redevelopment reducing the Colgate-Palmolive site from 23.5 acres to 7.25 acres.

From 1991 until 1997 a programme of continuous upgrading took place, once more transforming the place where so many local people have worked since the 1870s.

Top: The Colgate-Palmolive factory pictured in 2001.

Turning brass into gold

We all like brass. Especially the kind that goes in our pockets! But it's not just coins we like: brass beds and brass ornaments are as popular today as they ever were in the past. But brass is far more than being a simple adornment to our homes. This relatively soft and easily worked metal has thousands upon thousands of practical uses, and few mechanical objects in our homes and workplaces are without at least one brass component.

One local firm which knows more about brass than most of us is that of Donald Brown (Brownall) Ltd based in Stretford Road which has now been manufacturing brass products for almost a century.

The company was founded around 1914 by Mr Donald Brown as a Brass Machine Shop making various items for the Plumbing and Heating Engineering Industries. Around 1918 he was joined by a Mr Southall and it is believed that this led to the name 'Brownall' - a combination of the two men's names.

Below: *Staff pictured outside the works in 1947.*

The original premises for the company were on the first floor of Rastall's Foundry on Chester Road, and the company has always been located within a short distance of that original site.

At the time when the plumbing industry was changing over from using lead pipe, Donald Brown found a gap in the market to manufacture a range of reusable pipe fittings for copper. Other products included paraffin pourers, spray guns and gas light fittings. The company also developed a product range of its own including the Brownall swivel beer pipe fitting which was based on compression fittings suitable for use on 'monel' tube. This fitting enabled the publican to connect his beer pump to a group of barrels without moving any of them, simply by swivelling the pipe joint into position. There was also a range of barrel cocks and fittings for the beer trade.

From 1927 work was undertaken for the Vulcan Boiler Insurance Company and this included boiler fittings, fusible plugs and safety valves. These were the predecessors of the present day range of safety valves

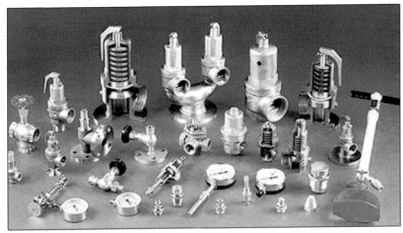

originally manufactured for the National Vulcan Insurance Company, which became the NABIC boiler valve products made today.

The company was incorporated as Donald Brown (Brownall) Ltd in 1935 and by 1938 the workforce had grown to about fifty and a move was made to the Lower Moss Lane Factory which had a foundry and machine shop on one site. This meant that for the first time the company was able to produce its own castings, a facility which it has retained to this day.

In 1946 Donald Brown sold out to the Vulcan Insurance Company and from 1950, following the appointment of a General Manager, Mr H G Wainwright, the company began to develop the famous Brownall laboratory taps. The current pipe fittings of the Brazoweld and Screwed product ranges also had their origins in the 1950s, when updated versions of some of the original products were introduced in their present form.

In 1977 the company moved to its present Stretford Road Premises, enabling expansion and further development of the existing products. During the long period of the company's existence there have been several take-overs by insurance companies and by the 1970s the ultimate parent company was Sun Alliance Insurance Group. It was decided in 1987 that an engineering manufacturing unit of this kind did not fit the profile of a

subsidiary for the Insurance Group and Donald Brown (Brownall) Ltd. was sold to Delta Engineering Holdings Limited on the 4th July 1988.

Following that take-over several additional products in the Heating and Ventilating Sector were introduced by the parent company and as a result Donald Brown would soon have product and marketing activities in three major product groups. These would be NABIC Boiler Safety Valves, Industrial Pipe Fittings and Heating, Ventilating and Water Valves. The current Brownall range of industrial pipe fittings are manufactured using the company's own in-house resources which include pattern making, casting and machining of components on the latest numerical control machine tools. These products have been developed over decades of practical use and testing with emphasis on reliability, ease of maintenance and practical design. A quality system to ISO 9001 standard ensures product quality is maintained at the highest level. By the opening years of the 21st century there are approximately 70 people on the site, working on all aspects of these product ranges from pattern making and foundry work through to machining and assembly, with a full range of supporting services such as design, sales and marketing and accounts.

The history of brass has a long way to go yet!

Top left: Some of the range of NABIC products, manufactured by the company. Above left: Brazoweld pipes. Below: The company premises.

Illuminating three generations

Electric lighting is a wonderful thing. The familiar electric light bulb was invented by Messrs. Joseph Swan and Thomas Edison in the closing years of Queen Victoria's reign. Since then the world has never looked the same - apart from wartime blackouts. In the early decades of the 20th century electric lighting began to quickly replace gas mantles, though many readers of this book will still dimly recall a gas lit youth.

Now, distributing the best and most exclusive designs of domestic lighting to selected retail outlets throughout Britain and Ireland, the Manchester based firm of JH Miller & Sons Limited had much more humble beginnings. The founder Joseph Hector Miller (1903-1978) was born in the Wirral, Cheshire, and throughout the 1920s and 1930s he was a salesman or agent for electric lamp manufacturers travelling all over the country. Those makers included such names from the past as Spero lamps, Atlas (which retailed at one shilling each, and were advertised as 'Bob Atlas') and Ekco lamps made by EK Cole who, memorably, also made radios. After wartime service with the Royal Engineers, Hector Miller decided that he would earn more money by running his own business. He would still sell lamp bulbs and the new fluorescent tubes but buy them directly from the makers - mainly Ismay - and sell them at negotiated prices mostly to 'big

users' the term used for mills, factories, warehouses and large hotels, but also to the retail trade.

Hector Miller soon realised that premises would be required and in 1949 he acquired a shop for use as a depot on Moss Lane West in Moss Side, right opposite Hyde's Brewery. The shop owner was formerly a customer of Hector's, selling his lamp bulbs, so it seemed obvious that this trade should be continued together with selling other electrical items such as plugs, cables and batteries. Hector's wife Dora, who had never worked in a shop before, was put in charge, with Hector helping out in the late afternoons and on Saturdays which were the busiest times. Before long light fittings, table lamps and floor standards were added to the range on offer, and all these items were sold to the retail customers. It was however the wholesale side of the business that prospered most and the trading name of JH Miller & Sons was adopted when Hector was joined by his sons, Bob (Robert) and Tony (Anthony), who would eventually succeed his father as company chairman.

It was quickly realised that running a wholesale business from a retail shop did not work well, so at the beginning

Top left: *Company founder Hector Miller.* **Above right:** *Robert (Bob) Miller.* **Right:** *The original premises in Hulme.*

Hulme. Then in November 1965 disaster struck when all the stock and offices were destroyed in a fire which had started in the basement and soon engulfed the floors above. It took twelve months to rebuild the premises and meanwhile temporary accommodation was found in nearby Ellesmere Street, but this was on the first floor and just not convenient. After returning to the rebuilt mill it was thought that would do for many years.

of 1953 the shop windows were painted over green with the name in gilt letters and 'Wholesale Only' painted on the doors. The shop next door was acquired, followed by an additional building on the opposite side of the road which included a useful loading bay; but before long it was realised that for further expansion to take place even better premises would have to be found.

At the end of the 1950s the firm took over the ground floor of an old cotton mill in Hulme Hall Road, in

Business however continued to expand and again it was found necessary to move. It was in October 1989 that JH Miller & Sons Ltd moved to its present premises, a modern industrial unit on Wardley Industrial Estate in Worsley. And perhaps now the company should be renamed JH Miller, Sons & Grandsons Ltd - with two of the third generation of the Miller family now with the firm. Today Tony's wife, Lesley, is company secretary, Bob's son, Richard, now a director and more recently Tony and Lesley's son, Simon, has become the latest family member to join the successful family business.

*Top left: Hector and Dora Miller. **Top right, both** pictures: Tony Miller and his wife Lesley. **Above left:** Richard Miller.*
Left: The modern company home in Worsley.
***Below:** Simon Miller.*

Beneath our feet

Do you ever wonder what lies in the earth under your home, office or factory? One local firm which could tell you the answer is Sub Soil Surveys Ltd.

Sub Soil Surveys Ltd was founded on 13th June 1956 by John Ingham and John Elkington. Both the company founders had worked together in the Royal Engineers serving as Garrison Engineers in Malaya between 1951 and 1954. Whilst stationed in Malaya the pair had the idea of one day forming a business specialising in drilling boreholes and undertaking geotechnical work.

The new business was established at 381 Bury New Road, Prestwich. The small firm shared ground floor office accommodation with an estate agents and took over the cellar for use as a small laboratory for soil analysis.

In those less regulated post war years problems could often be solved using unconventional means. In 1957 near Criccieth, North Wales, whilst attempting to sink boreholes through very difficult strata consisting mainly of boulders and large cobbles, progress ground to a halt in spite of extensive heavy chiselling. In order to reach the required depths it was decided to help things along by the use of explosives. Fortunately a nearby explosives manufacturing plant was able to oblige, and with some trial and error it was found possible to shatter the obstructions and thus complete the boreholes to the necessary depth. It is rather unlikely that such an informal approach could be used these days!

In the years at Prestwich the staff consisted of no more than the two founders together with Mrs Elkington, along with an occasional labourer to help with the single drill rig. Most of the drilling work, initially intermittent, was carried out by the two directors who did the office and laboratory work during quiet periods.

Contracts were generally small ones but the company was able to slowly expand, securing ever larger contracts, many from Local Authorities.

Eventually a larger building was needed together with a compound where the drilling equipment could be kept. In 1959 the company moved to its present home in Kennedy Road, Astley.

Following the early death of John Elkington in 1959, Dr John Alderman joined the Company in 1960 and became equal partner with John Ingham in Sub Soil Surveys Limited.

Dr John Alderman, after graduation with 1st Class Honours in Civil Engineering at Manchester University, gained his practical experience at the Building Research Station, before being invited by Prof. Gibson to join the Lecturing and Research Staff at Manchester University. His main task was to start a course in "Soil Mechanics" which was a new subject in the Civil Engineers training. During his 12 years at the University, Dr Alderman obtained MSc and PhD degrees for his Soil Mechanics research, in particular on the Geotechnical problems of Glacial Deposits in the North-West. He also introduced "Concrete Technology" and "Highway Engineering" into the University syllabus, and is a Member of the Institute of Highway Engineers. As a Geotechnical Consultant he was

Above centre: Rotary drilling during the 1960s.
Below: Laboratory Assistant taking a dry weight for sulphate content test. Below left: A technician checking pore water pressure apparatus, circa 1960.

Both new companies operated from the same premises at Astley, the former being responsible for laboratory and in situ testing of soils and materials, the latter for the compilation of geotechnical reports together with advice and recommendations on a variety of soil and foundation problems.

Since the company's birth the extent and type of services undertaken has grown considerably; for example following the increasing use of 'Brown-field' building sites considerable emphasis began to be placed on investigations to determine the type and degree of contamination which might be present.

Environmental considerations apart, much emphasis would also be placed on the ability of investigation services to operate in urban and industrial locations which frequently call for boreholes and tests within buildings and confined spaces. This would lead to the need for specialised small light rigs and equipment and, more importantly, drilling crews and a staff sufficiently experienced to get the best out of such operations.

Throughout the life of the company it has been its policy to promote continuity of employment and to enlarge employees experience. The success of that policy is self evident; at the start of the new millennium the longest serving member being Alan Roddy, Laboratory Manager, who joined the firm in

involved in investigating sites with difficult foundation problems and in associate legal cases and arbitrations, etc.

In order to meet increasing technical demands Sub Soil Testing Ltd was established in 1972 for the testing of soils, concrete and other materials and this was followed in 1986 by Sub Soil Consultancy Services Ltd when Richard Shires became the 3rd Director, and later its Managing Director. Following an Honours Degree at UMIST, and after gaining contracting and consulting experience he joined Sub Soil Surveys Ltd in 1978 and became a Chartered Civil Engineer in 1981. Since then the Consulting Service has expanded from the core Geotechnical work to encompass the whole Geoenvironmental field.

This page: Just some of the great variety of investigations - totalling approximately 10,000, that the firm has undertaken since 1956.

1963, whilst W Patrick, Drilling Manager, notched up 36 years of service. Cliff Pritchard, formerly Drilling Foreman, now Storekeeper, started in 1974. JFR Ingham commenced with the Company in 1986 and is currently employed as Contracts Manager.

Not odd at all

The institutions which today we take for granted, such as the National Health Service, did not always exist. Unemployment and sickness benefit and old age pensions only came into being during the early 20th century. How did people cope? One answer was the Oddfellows.

The Oddfellows remains a mutual non-profit making friendly society with the aim of ensuring members join together to enjoy the social side of life, alongside providing care and support in times of need. The Oddfellows has no political or religious affiliations and membership is open to all regardless of age, sex, political persuasion, religion, race, colour or disability.

The history of the Oddfellows dates back officially to its founding in the streets of Manchester in 1810: its roots however go back several centuries before then.

The name Oddfellows can be traced back to the 14th century at the time of the Trade Guilds. 'Odd Fellows' came to represent a mix of Guildsmen from a variety of trades who banded together for common protection and support.

Around 1808 Robert Naylor, who later became Grand Master (Chairman), started a social and benevolent club based at the Ropemaker's Arms, in Chapel Street, Salford. It was very successful and was soon joined by a large contingent of members from the Prince Regent Lodge of Oddfellows of the Sheffield United Order. The first meeting of this amalgamated society was on 10th October 1810 at the Robin Hood Hotel in Church Street, Manchester. This has become the official founding day of

Above: An artist's impression of the Grosvenor Street premises. Below: The Grand-Master's Church Parade outside the Oddfellows Hall, Bridge Street, Ramsbottom.

the Independent Order of Oddfellows, Manchester Unity Friendly Society (the Society's registered name). With improved organisation and rules they encouraged many other lodges to join them with their names often evoking recollections of their origins such as the Poor Man's Protection Lodge of Boothstown, the Earl of Durham Lodge in Hulme and the Joseph Berry Lodge in Swinton.

In 1857 permission was granted for the Oddfellows to build their own offices in Grosvenor Street. The following is an extract taken from the Oddfellow Magazine printed that year:

'Several gentlemen sent in plans of their plots, and the directors inspected them. After viewing them all they subsequently came to the conclusion to purchase the land and buildings in Grosvenor Street...The architect chosen was Mr Joseph Lindley of Ashton-under-Lyne and Mr Penk of Manchester was the fortunate individual on whom has devolved the building of the offices.

The foundation stone to the new offices... was laid with this trowel by James Charles Cox, Esq., of Southampton on the 19th February 1857. In the stone were deposited the following documents:- Copy of minute book, 1814; list of lodges 1857; general laws, ditto; a bottle containing the

names of the officers of the Order, board of directors and trustees; a number of coins of the present reign; Manchester and Liverpool newspapers of the day; copy of American covenant of Oddfellowship 1838 and a list of the toast to be given at the dinner in celebration of the event.'

Soon Manchester residents would become familiar with the neo-classical frontage of the friendly society's offices with its distinctive arched windows and doorway, a building which reflected the growing prestige of the Oddfellows.

By 1850 the Oddfellows had already become the largest and richest friendly society in Britain. This growth was spurred by the Industrial Revolution - as people streamed into towns and cities to work, the need for mutual protection was soon apparent.

In the 1937/8 'Official Handbook and Directory' for the Manchester District there were 31 lodges listed. Members would meet in hotels in places such as Droylsden, Openshaw, Salford, Boothstown, Gorton, Hulme, Patricroft, Newton Heath, Pendleton, Rhodes and Denton. Many of the early lodges met in taverns or pubs which is why so many pubs in Britain today are named the Oddfellows or the Oddfellows Arms; invariably these are past meeting places of lodges.

Today the Oddfellows' offices are located in a new property built for them in 1967 in Fountain Street. They are still one of the largest branch based friendly societies and continue to innovate - developing new and improved services to support members. Many of the 250 branches have active social programmes and all provide help and support to members in the local areas around the country.

*Above: Some pages from the Independent Order of Odd Fellows annual newsletters. **Left:** Oddfellows Hall, now home to the English Language faculty of UMIST.*

Fresh food daily

There's many a good business story about a man who starts with nothing more than a small market stall but is blessed with unstoppable ambition. The story of local catering supply firm R Noone & Son Ltd is almost like that, but with one important distinction - in this case it was a lady who had the stall.

Rose Noone founded the business in the late 1960s after having previously worked in a variety of jobs, including working in factories and in the retail trade.

The firm began on a market stall in Heywood, selling fruit and vegetables, where Rose worked for Stan Cowell before she bought the business for £400. Having a fruit and veg stall looks like a grand life; many readers will be envious of those who work for themselves, and if they shut their eyes can even smell the glorious scents thrown up by boxes of oranges and apples.

But of course in truth it is very hard work; stall holders need to be up well before the crack of dawn to get their produce at the wholesale markets. And if the day starts early it finishes late too with the books to be done each evening. Fortunately Rose was up to the challenge, but there is no doubt she would have welcomed a little extra help. Fortunately before too long she got it.

Rose's son Michael left the Royal navy in 1976 and joined his mother who promptly made him a partner. Rose's two daughters, Tracey and Susan, both joined the business in the mid 1980s. Whilst Mike Noone did the buying at the wholesale markets Rose, Tracey and Susan now ran a shop.

The market stall had been sold and the business expanded by moving into the high street, first to a shop in Heywood, then another in Middleton which became very successful, not least when fresh fish was added to the fruit and vegetables for sale.

Another shop was opened in the Middleton Arndale Centre in 1988 and in 1990 one in Sale, Cheshire.

Below: *A view of the front of the Middleton shop.*

The shops however came under increasing pressure from supermarkets in the mid 1990s, especially after the Sunday opening laws were changed. The shop in Sale was sold in 1995 and the company changed direction and entered the catering supply business.

Soon the firm's main customers would no longer be the individual housewife but the UK's catering industry with restaurants, cafés, canteens, sandwich bars and even nursing homes becoming the business' mainstays.

But if the customers were changing the quality produce was not, with fruit and vegetables and fresh fish as good as ever but now being supplemented by dairy produce - cheese, milk and cream. And with sales limited to within just 20 miles of the

firm's base a consistently excellent service was assured. The survival and growth of the business over the years was built on quality, service and value - and, wholesale or retail, those values have been equally applied, with decades of experience in sourcing the best quality products to benefit customers every day.

R Noone & Son Ltd intends to continue with its winning formula: first rate produce and an unbeatable service. But it would not only be the quality of its produce and service which has ensured that the company has prospered. The business has been fortunate to retain members of staff for long periods, and they would be a cornerstone of the firm's success. Andy Clark for example has worked for the firm for over 20 years, since he left school, to eventually become Noone's Administration Manager for its Wholesale Division. Similarly Lynne Caine has worked for the business for over 15 years to become its Retail Manager. Yet another Noone stalwart has been Lee McGuiness who, with 10 years under his belt since leaving school, became Warehouse Manager for the Wholesale Division .

The next generation is growing fast in the shape of Mike and Maggie's own family, Lucy, Francesca and Phillipa. This company is, and intends to remain, a family business; its welcome philosophy - loyalty to its staff and customers, and an equal value placed on the loyalty of its customers to the firm - is, in an age more noted for discourtesy and little apparent interest in staff or customers, a shining example for others to emulate.   .

This: *An interior and exterior view of the Middleton shop.*

Residents of Rosamund Street, Chorlton on Medlock, celebrate VE Day.

Acknowledgments

The publishers would like to thank

Manchester Central Library - Archive and Local Studies Unit - for providing all the editorial images that have appeared in this publication.

Paula Moorhouse

Andrew Mitchell

Steve Ainsworth

True North Books Ltd - Book List

Memories of Accrington - 1 903204 05 4

Memories of Barnet - 1 903204 16 X

Memories of Barnsley - 1 900463 11 3

Golden Years of Barnsley -1 900463 87 3

Memories of Basingstoke - 1 903204 26 7

Memories of Bedford - 1 900463 83 0

More Memories of Bedford - 1 903204 33 X

Golden Years of Birmingham - 1 900463 04 0

Birmingham Memories - 1 903204 45 3

Memories of Blackburn - 1 900463 40 7

More Memories of Blackburn - 1 900463 96 2

Memories of Blackpool - 1 900463 21 0

Memories of Bolton - 1 900463 45 8

More Memories of Bolton - 1 900463 13 X

Bolton Memories - 1 903204 37 2

Memories of Bournemouth -1 900463 44 X

Memories of Bradford - 1 900463 00 8

More Memories of Bradford - 1 900463 16 4

More Memories of Bradford II - 1 900463 63 6

Bradford Memories - 1 903204 47 X

Bradford City Memories - 1 900463 57 1

Memories of Bristol - 1 900463 78 4

More Memories of Bristol - 1 903204 43 7

Memories of Bromley - 1 903204 21 6

Memories of Burnley - 1 900463 95 4

Golden Years of Burnley - 1 900463 67 9

Memories of Bury - 1 900463 90 3

Memories of Cambridge - 1 900463 88 1

Memories of Cardiff - 1 900463 14 8

Memories of Carlisle - 1 900463 38 5

Memories of Chelmsford - 1 903204 29 1

Memories of Cheltenham - 1 903204 17 8

Memories of Chester - 1 900463 46 6

More Memories of Chester -1 903204 02 X

Memories of Chesterfield -1 900463 61 X

More Memories of Chesterfield - 1 903204 28 3

Memories of Colchester - 1 900463 74 1

Nostalgic Coventry - 1 900463 58 X

Coventry Memories - 1 903204 38 0

Memories of Croydon - 1 900463 19 9

More Memories of Croydon - 1 903204 35 6

Golden Years of Darlington - 1 900463 72 5

Nostalgic Darlington - 1 900463 31 8

Darlington Memories - 1 903204 46 1

Memories of Derby - 1 900463 37 7

More Memories of Derby - 1 903204 20 8

Memories of Dewsbury & Batley - 1 900463 80 6

Memories of Doncaster - 1 900463 36 9

Nostalgic Dudley - 1 900463 03 2

Memories of Edinburgh - 1 900463 33 4

Memories of Enfield - 1 903204 14 3

Memories of Exeter - 1 900463 94 6

Memories of Glasgow - 1 900463 68 7

More Memories of Glasgow - 1 903204 44 5

Memories of Gloucester - 1 903204 04 6

Memories of Grimsby - 1 900463 97 0

More Memories of Grimsby - 1 903204 36 4

Memories of Guildford - 1 903204 22 4

Memories of Halifax - 1 900463 05 9

More Memories of Halifax - 1 900463 06 7

Golden Years of Halifax - 1 900463 62 8

Nostalgic Halifax - 1 903204 30 5

Memories of Harrogate - 1 903204 01 1

Memories of Hartlepool - 1 900463 42 3

Memories of High Wycombe - 1 900463 84 9

Memories of Huddersfield - 1 900463 15 6

More Memories of Huddersfield - 1 900463 26 1

Golden Years of Huddersfield - 1 900463 77 6

Nostalgic Huddersfield - 1 903204 19 4

Huddersfield Town FC - 1 900463 51 2

Memories of Hull - 1 900463 86 5

More Memories of Hull - 1 903204 06 2

Memories of Ipswich - 1 900463 09 1

More Memories of Ipswich - 1 903204 52 6

Memories of Keighley - 1 900463 01 6

Golden Years of Keighley - 1 900463 92 X

Memories of Kingston - 1 903204 24 0

Memories of Leeds - 1 900463 75 X

Continued overleaf

True North Books Ltd - Book List

More Memories of Leeds - 1 900463 12 1

Golden Years of Leeds - 1 903204 07 0

Memories of Leicester - 1 900463 08 3

More Memories of Leicester - 1 903204 08 9

Memories of Leigh - 1 903204 27 5

Memories of Lincoln - 1 900463 43 1

Memories of Liverpool - 1 900463 07 5

More Memories of Liverpool - 1 903204 09 7

Liverpool Memories - 1 903204 53 4

Memories of Luton - 1 900463 93 8

Memories of Macclesfield - 1 900463 28 8

Memories of Manchester - 1 900463 27 X

More Memories of Manchester - 1 903204 03 8

Manchester Memories - 1 903204 54 2

Memories of Middlesbrough - 1 900463 56 3

More Memories of Middlesbrough - 1 903204 42 9

Memories of Newbury - 1 900463 79 2

Memories of Newcastle - 1 900463 81 4

More Memories of Newcastle - 1 903204 10 0

Memories of Newport - 1 900463 59 8

Memories of Northampton - 1 900463 48 2

More Memories of Northampton - 1 903204 34 8

Memories of Norwich - 1 900463 73 3

Memories of Nottingham - 1 900463 91 1

More Memories of Nottingham - 1 903204 11 9

Bygone Oldham - 1 900463 25 3

Memories of Oldham - 1 900463 76 8

Memories of Oxford - 1 900463 54 7

Memories of Peterborough - 1 900463 98 9

Golden Years of Poole - 1 900463 69 5

Memories of Portsmouth - 1 900463 39 3

More Memories of Portsmouth - 1 903204 51 8

Nostalgic Preston - 1 900463 50 4

More Memories of Preston - 1 900463 17 2

Preston Memories - 1 903204 41 0

Memories of Reading - 1 900463 49 0

Memories of Rochdale - 1 900463 60 1

More Memories of Reading - 1 903204 39 9

More Memories of Rochdale - 1 900463 22 9

Memories of Romford - 1 903204 40 2

Memories of St Albans - 1 903204 23 2

Memories of St Helens - 1 900463 52 0

Memories of Sheffield - 1 900463 20 2

More Memories of Sheffield - 1 900463 32 6

Golden Years of Sheffield - 1 903204 13 5

Memories of Slough - 1 900 463 29 6

Golden Years of Solihull - 1 903204 55 0

Memories of Southampton - 1 900463 34 2

More Memories of Southampton - 1 903204 49 6

Memories of Stockport - 1 900463 55 5

More Memories of Stockport - 1 903204 18 6

Memories of Stockton - 1 900463 41 5

Memories of Stoke-on-Trent - 1 900463 47 4

More Memories of Stoke-on-Trent - 1 903204 12 7

Memories of Stourbridge - 1903204 31 3

Memories of Sunderland - 1 900463 71 7

More Memories of Sunderland - 1 903204 48 8

Memories of Swindon - 1 903204 00 3

Memories of Uxbridge - 1 900463 64 4

Memories of Wakefield - 1 900463 65 2

More Memories of Wakefield - 1 900463 89 X

Nostalgic Walsall - 1 900463 18 0

Golden Years of Walsall - 1 903204 56 9

More Memories of Warrington - 1 900463 02 4

Memories of Watford - 1 900463 24 5

Golden Years of West Bromwich - 1 900463 99 7

Memories of Wigan - 1 900463 85 7

Golden Years of Wigan - 1 900463 82 2

Nostalgic Wirral - 1 903204 15 1

Memories of Woking - 1 903204 32 1

Nostalgic Wolverhampton - 1 900463 53 9

Wolverhampton Memories - 1 903204 50 X

Memories of Worcester - 1 903204 25 9

Memories of Wrexham - 1 900463 23 7

Memories of York - 1 900463 66 0